PIECED TO FIT

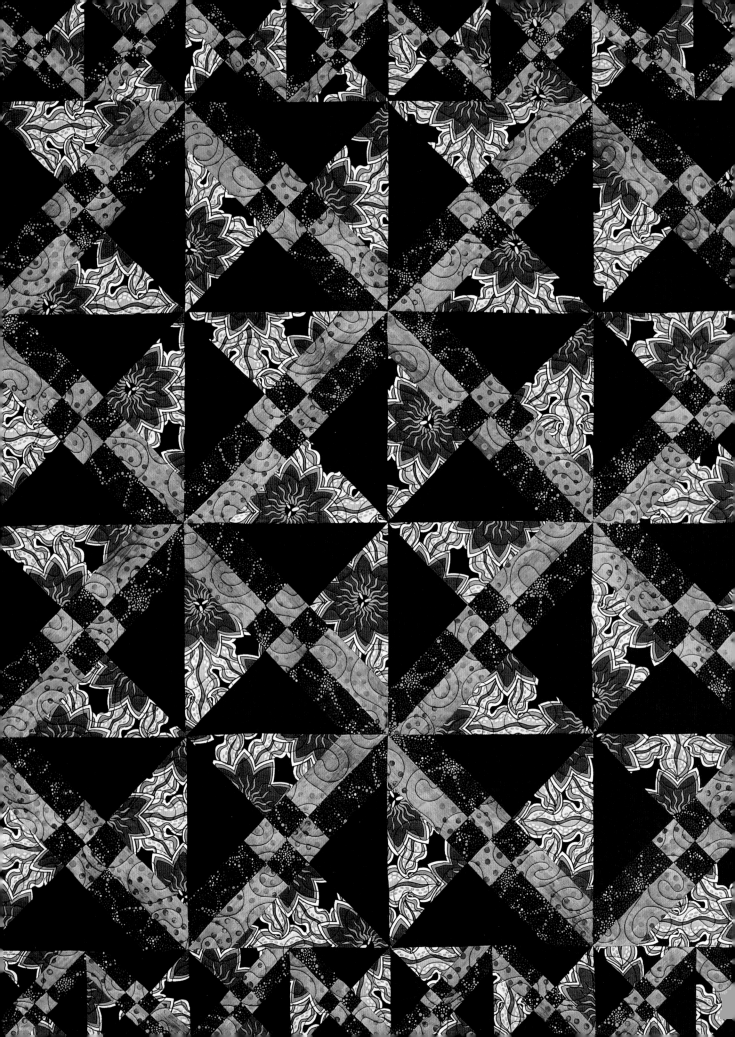

Pieced to Fit

Instant Quilt Borders from Easy Blocks

Sheila Sinclair Snyder

Martingale®

& COMPANY

Pieced to Fit:
Instant Quilt Borders from Easy Blocks
© 2004 by Sheila Sinclair Snyder

That Patchwork Place® is an imprint of
Martingale & Company®.

Martingale & Company
20205 144th Avenue NE
Woodinville, WA 98072-8478 USA
www.martingale-pub.com

Printed in China
09 08 07 06 05 04   8 7 6 5 4 3 2 1

Library of Congress Cataloging-in-Publication Data

Snyder, Sheila Sinclair.
    Pieced to fit : instant quilt borders from easy blocks / Sheila Sinclair Snyder.
        p. cm.
    ISBN 1-56477-561-5
1. Patchwork—Patterns. 2. Machine quilting—Patterns. I. Title.
    TT835.S62 2004
    746.46'041—dc22
                                    2004012861

Credits

President ▪ Nancy J. Martin
CEO ▪ Daniel J. Martin
Publisher ▪ Jane Hamada
Editorial Director ▪ Mary V. Green
Managing Editor ▪ Tina Cook
Technical Editor ▪ Darra Williamson
Copy Editor ▪ Melissa Bryan
Design Director ▪ Stan Green
Illustrator ▪ Robin Strobel
Cover and Text Designer ▪ Shelly Garrison
Photographer ▪ Brent Kane

Mission Statement

Dedicated to providing quality products
and service to inspire creativity.

DEDICATION

To Matthew and Julia. You have always been my inspiration.
To my parents, Dean and Patricia Sinclair, who could do anything, and made me think that I could too.

ACKNOWLEDGMENTS

I am grateful to have had the support and help of many generous people while preparing this book. Thank heaven for friends!

My husband, Elvin, came to the rescue by cutting strips and bringing home dinner when he realized I had stopped cooking! It's amazing how much he has learned about quilts over the years.

My sister, Sandy Fuhr, used her writing skills to develop my elementary comments into cohesive introductions. Although she isn't an active quilter, she's interested enough to ask good questions.

Judy Dillree, Sally Franzoni, Yolaine Adams, Lorraine Gard, Marie Dickes, Margaret Wells, and Betty Critzer all helped with time-consuming handwork so that I could focus on larger tasks.

A special thank you to my "sisters" in the neighborhood, Ellie Abarr and Marie Dickes, who made sure I was making progress, offered all kinds of help, and stopped in to share the news or a laugh on a regular basis.

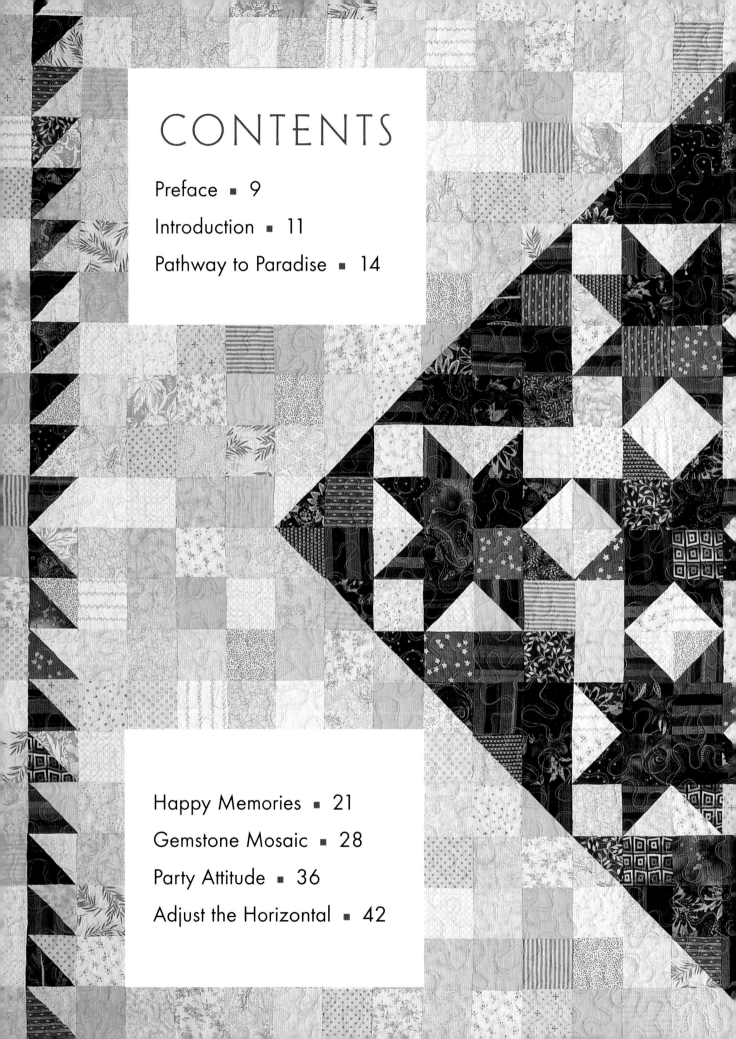

CONTENTS

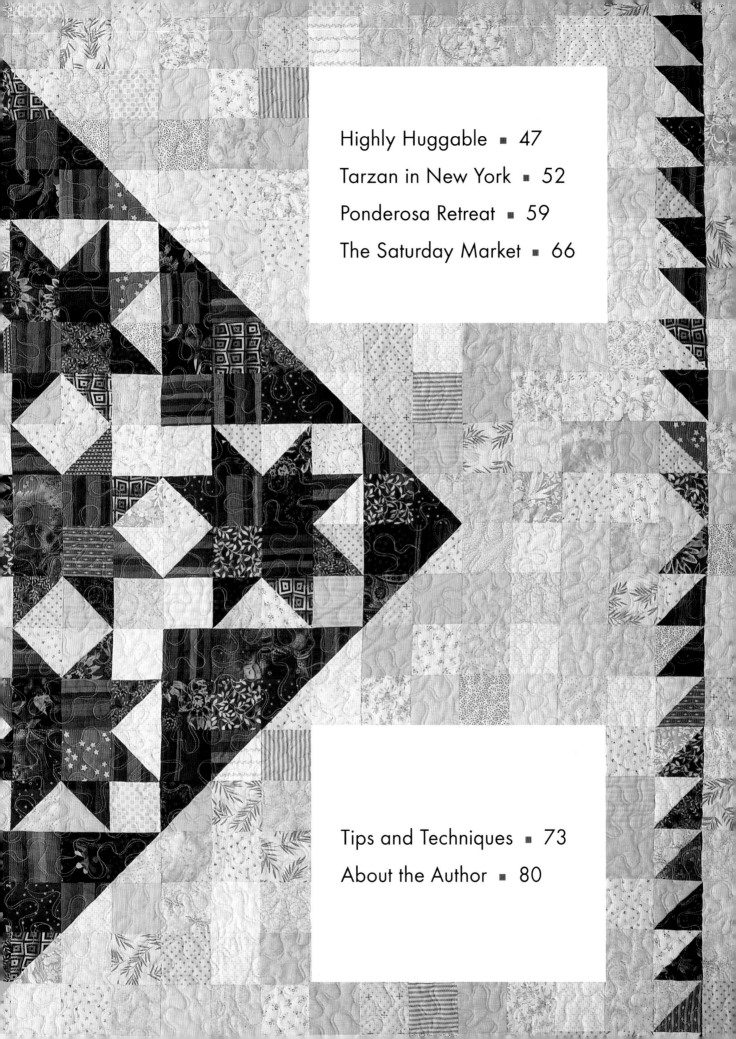

PREFACE

I grew up on the Minnesota prairie seeing long, unobstructed horizons and beautifully colored sunsets. The northern lights were a marvel in the fall. I was instilled with a sense of unlimited possibilities, a love of beauty, and a sense of wonder for color and how colors work together. In my family, we valued doing things with our own two hands as well as figuring things out one step at a time. Everything we did—whether gardening, farming, raising animals, building fences, fixing equipment, woodworking, sewing, cooking, or simply playing together—was done with creativity and pride.

It was natural for me to take up quilting with my grandmother. She was a quilter and seamstress with an indispensable strength: the ability to create while caring for a big family, fitting her stitching in amidst the daily work. The members of my family have many talents, including leadership, writing, music, weaving, woodworking, scrapbooking, knitting, and cross-stitch. At the moment, I am the only active quilter, but I'm working on them!

I am constantly intrigued by the multiple layers of design that make up a completed quilt. The block or appliqué design, the texture and pattern of the fabric, the colors and their interplay, the dimension of the quilting, the quilting design and thread color, and even the way the quilt will be used are all elements of the design. With choices to be made at every level of design, no wonder we are fascinated! My hope is that we will continue to discover new ways to think about quilting, design, construction, and tools, and that the connections made with quilters and other artists will continue to enrich our lives.

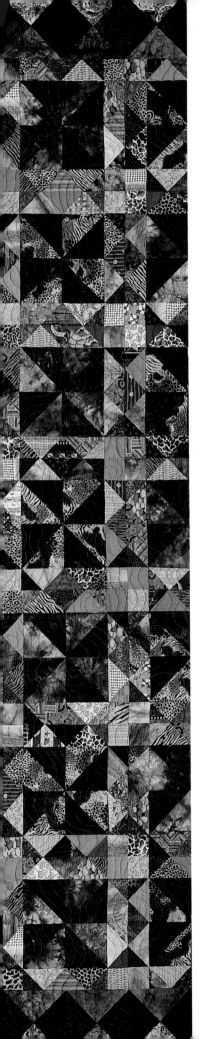

INTRODUCTION

This book was inspired by my customers and the work I do as a professional machine quilter. I am constantly exposed to new patterns, fabrics, combinations, and creativity. My customers have become my friends, and they freely share the zeal and excitement they have for quilting.

One thing quilters love is choice—the more choices, the better! I developed the series of quilts featured in this book to offer another choice in how we think about borders and sashing.

The first five quilts focus on borders, border effects, and designs that provide a finished look without the need to attach a separate border. We all know that plain borders can become difficult to manage and apply smoothly. The pieced borders I've used here are constructed as blocks, all of a manageable size. The quilt assembly is simplified because the border blocks are sewn at the same time as the rows of blocks in the center of the quilt.

The second half of the book focuses on an alternate way to think of sashing—more choices! These designs use the sashing as an integral part of the block, more so than as simple spacing between the blocks. The sashing is incorporated into the block design and becomes apparent when the blocks are joined, creating a wonderful overall pattern.

Borders Made from Blocks

"Happy Memories," "Party Attitude," and "Adjust the Horizontal" display examples of borders constructed as blocks.

Borders Created through Color Placement

"Pathway to Paradise" and "Gemstone Mosaic" offer another choice. The outer blocks in these quilts are colored in a way that creates the illusion of a border, giving the quilt a finished appearance.

Sashing Incorporated into Block Design

Examples of incorporated sashing are the trees and nine-patch elements of "Ponderosa Retreat," the playfulness of "Highly Huggable," and the geometry of "The Saturday Market."

Sashing and Border Combined

Finally, "Tarzan in New York" combines the sashing and border ideas for even more choices!

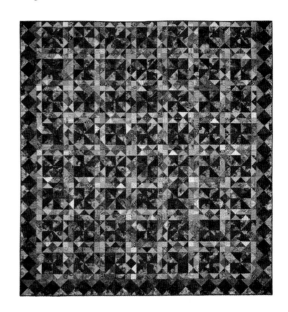

PATHWAY TO PARADISE

There's a glowing hedge around this not-so-secret garden paradise. The central medallion, reminiscent of a Hawaiian appliqué quilt, has been tamed and kept to size by the tropical interior border. A saucy snakelike trail dances its way through the blues to give this quilt a finished look without the need for added borders.

MATERIALS

Yardage amounts are based on 42"-wide fabric.

- 5¼ yards of dark blue print for Pathway and Flower blocks
- 2 yards of medium blue print for Pathway and Flower blocks
- 1½ yards of lime green solid for Flower blocks
- ⅞ yard of medium-light green multicolored print for appliqué background
- ⅞ yard of dark blue plaid for appliqués
- ⅝ yard of medium aqua print for Pathway blocks
- ⅝ yard of medium-light aqua print for Pathway blocks
- ½ yard of light blue print for Flower blocks
- ⅜ yard *each* of 2 different medium yellow prints for Flower blocks*
- 9 yards of fabric for backing
- ¾ yard of dark blue fabric for binding
- 102" x 102" piece of batting

If you prefer scrappy yellow flower centers, simply use 80 yellow squares, 2½" x 2½", to make the four-patch units.

CUTTING

All cutting instructions include ¼"-wide seam allowances. Refer to page 16 for appliqué cutting instructions.

From the dark blue plaid, cut:
4 squares, 14" x 14"

From the medium-light green multicolored print, cut:
4 squares, 14" x 14"

From the dark blue print, cut:
30 strips, 3½" x 42"; crosscut 15 strips into 160 squares, 3½" x 3½". Set the remaining strips aside.

16 strips, 2" x 42"

10 strips, 4½" x 42"; crosscut into 80 squares, 4½" x 4½"

DESIGNER'S TIP
"Pathway to Paradise" is a good example of a quilt that can become heavy due to its size, the weight of the thread, and numerous seam allowances. I used wool batting to avoid adding unnecessary weight. As an added plus, I gained the benefits of wool: warmth, a nice drape, and easy needling.

Finished quilt size: 96" x 96" ■ Finished block size: 12" square

Pieced and machine quilted by Sheila Sinclair Snyder. Appliqué completed by Judy Dillree.

From the medium blue print, cut:

15 strips, 3½" x 42"

5 strips, 2½" x 42"

From the medium aqua print, cut:

8 strips, 2" x 42"

From the medium-light aqua print, cut:

8 strips, 2" x 42"

From the lime green solid, cut:

20 strips, 2½" x 42"; crosscut 10 strips into 160 squares, 2½" x 2½". Set the remaining strips aside.

From the light blue print, cut:

5 strips, 2½" x 42"

From *each* medium yellow print, cut:

3 strips, 2½" x 42" (6 total)

From the dark blue fabric for binding, cut:

10 strips, 2¼" x 42"

MAKING THE BLOCKS

You need three different types of blocks to construct this quilt: four appliqué blocks, 40 Pathway blocks, and 20 Flower blocks.

Appliqué Blocks

Follow the instructions on pages 73–75 in "Tips and Techniques" or use your favorite method of appliqué. I chose the needle-turn appliqué method for my quilt because I felt it best suited the formality of this project.

1. Use the pattern on page 20 to make a template for piece A. Trace the template onto a 14" dark blue plaid square. Cut out the appliqué, adding the necessary seam allowance.

2. Center the A piece on a 14" medium-light green multicolored square. Refer to the quilt photo on page 15 for guidance as needed.

3. Appliqué the design to the background.

4. Trim the block to 12½" x 12½".

5. Repeat steps 1–4 to make a total of four appliqué blocks.

Pathway Blocks

1. Sew a 3½"-wide dark blue strip to a 3½"-wide medium blue strip along one long edge; press. Make 15 strip sets. Crosscut the strip sets into 160 segments, 3½" wide.

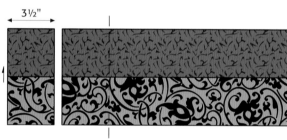

Make 15 strip sets.
Cut 160 segments.

2. Arrange and sew two segments from step 1 to make a four-patch unit as shown; press. Make 80.

  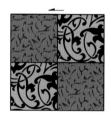

Make 80.

3. Sew a 2"-wide medium aqua strip to a 2"-wide dark blue strip along one long edge; press. Make eight strip sets. Crosscut the strip sets into 160 segments, 2" wide.

 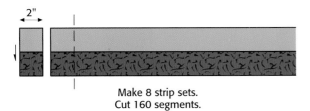

Make 8 strip sets.
Cut 160 segments.

4. Arrange and sew two segments from step 3 to make a four-patch unit as shown; press. Make 80.

Make 80.

5. Sew a 2"-wide medium-light aqua strip to a 2"-wide dark blue strip along one long edge; press. Make eight strip sets. Crosscut the strip sets into 160 segments, 2" wide.

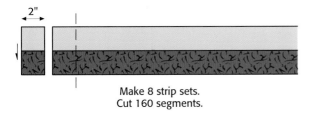

Make 8 strip sets.
Cut 160 segments.

6. Arrange and sew two segments from step 5 to make a four-patch unit as shown; press. Make 80.

Make 80.

7. Arrange and sew two 3½" dark blue squares, a four-patch unit from step 4, and a four-patch unit from step 6 as shown; press. Make 80.

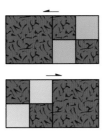 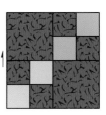 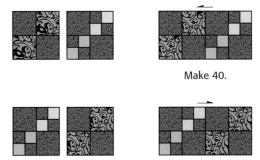

Make 80.

8. Sew each unit from step 7 to a four-patch unit from step 2, carefully arranging the colors as shown; press. Make 40 of each arrangement.

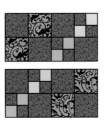

Make 40.

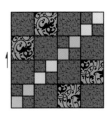

Make 40.

9. Arrange and sew two units from step 8, one of each color arrangement, as shown; press. The small four-patches will form a pathway diagonally through the block. Make 40 blocks.

Make 40.

Flower Blocks

1. Draw a diagonal line on the wrong side of each 2½" lime green square. Place a marked square right sides together with one corner of a 4½" dark blue square. Stitch on the drawn line. Trim the excess seam allowance to ¼"; press. Repeat to sew a marked lime green square to an adjacent corner of the blue square; trim and press. Make 80.

Make 80.

2. Sew a 2½"-wide lime green strip to a 2½"-wide medium blue strip along one long edge; press. Make five strip sets. Crosscut the strip sets into 80 segments, 2½" wide.

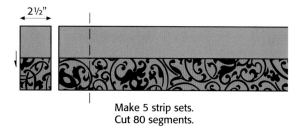

Make 5 strip sets.
Cut 80 segments.

3. Sew a 2½"-wide lime green strip to a 2½"-wide light blue strip along one long edge; press. Make five strip sets. Crosscut the strip sets into 80 segments, 2½" wide.

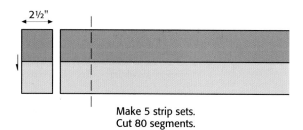

Make 5 strip sets.
Cut 80 segments.

4. Arrange and sew one segment each from step 2 and step 3 to make a four-patch unit as shown; press. Make 80.

Make 80.

5. Sew a 2½"-wide medium yellow strip to a contrasting 2½"-wide medium yellow strip along one long edge; press. Make three strip sets, pressing all seams toward the same fabric. Crosscut the strip sets into 40 segments, 2½" wide.

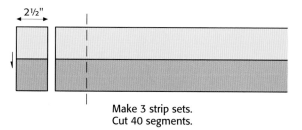

Make 3 strip sets.
Cut 40 segments.

6. Arrange and sew two segments from step 5 to make a four-patch unit as shown; press. Make 20.

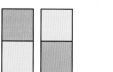

Make 20.

7. Arrange four units from step 1, four units from step 4, and a unit from step 6 as shown. Sew the units into rows; press. Sew the rows together; press. Make 20 blocks.

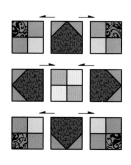
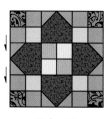

Make 20.

ASSEMBLING THE QUILT

1. Arrange the blocks in eight rows of eight blocks each, referring to the quilt plan below for guidance. Pay special attention to the correct orientation of the Pathway blocks.

2. Sew the blocks together into rows. Press the seams in opposite directions from row to row.

3. Sew the rows together; press.

FINISHING THE QUILT

1. Divide the backing fabric crosswise into three equal pieces. Remove the selvage and sew the pieces together to make a single backing piece with two horizontal seams.

2. Layer the quilt top, batting, and backing; baste. (Professional machine quilters prefer to receive the quilt unbasted.)

3. Quilt as desired by hand or machine. I used an allover blossom design for this quilt.

4. Referring to pages 77–78 of "Tips and Techniques," use the 2¼"-wide dark blue strips to bind your quilt.

5. Add a hanging sleeve and a label as described on pages 78–79.

Quilt Plan

Make 4.

Flip pattern along this line.

Center

Flip pattern along this line.

Piece A
Cut 4.

HAPPY MEMORIES

Carol Vogt was my red-haired best friend from high school, with whom I learned tailoring in home economics class. For the wool coat assignment—a necessity in Minnesota—Carol chose purple, and I settled on khaki. Those coats went to Goodwill long ago, but choosing and working with the colors for this quilt triggered many happy memories of adventures Carol and I had together. This design is dedicated to Carol, to our friendship, and to her beautiful daughters: Sonia, Heidi, and Crystal.

MATERIALS

Yardage amounts are based on 42"-wide fabric.

- 4⅛ yards of green print for Time and Tide blocks, border blocks, and binding
- 1½ yards of light background print #1 for Time and Tide blocks
- 1¼ yards of multicolored focus print for Time and Tide blocks and border blocks
- 1¼ yards of purple print for Time and Tide blocks and border blocks
- 1¼ yards of light background print #2 for border blocks
- 5 yards of fabric for backing
- 78" x 90" piece of batting

CUTTING

All cutting instructions include ¼"-wide seam allowances.

From the purple print, cut:

2 strips, 5¼" x 42"; crosscut into 10 squares, 5¼" x 5¼"

6 strips, 4¾" x 42"; crosscut 3 strips into 22 squares, 4¾" x 4¾". Set the remaining strips aside.

From the multicolored focus print, cut:

2 strips, 5¼" x 42"; crosscut into 10 squares, 5¼" x 5¼"

6 strips, 4¾" x 42"; crosscut 3 strips into 22 squares, 4¾" x 4¾". Set the remaining strips aside.

From the light background print #1, cut:

10 strips, 4¾" x 42"

From the green print, cut:

7 strips, 5⅛" x 42"; crosscut into 80 rectangles, 3¼" x 5⅛". Cut 40 of the rectangles in half diagonally to make 80 A triangles and cut the remaining 40 diagonally *in the opposite direction* to make 80 A reverse triangles.

6 strips, 5⅜" x 42"; crosscut into 80 rectangles, 2¾" x 5⅜". Cut 40 of the rectangles in half diagonally to make 80 C triangles and cut the remaining 40 diagonally *in the opposite direction* to make 80 C reverse triangles.

4 strips, 12½" x 42"; crosscut into 40 strips, 3½" x 12½"

2 strips, 3½" x 42"; crosscut into 4 strips, 3½" x 9½", and 4 squares, 3½" x 3½"

9 strips, 2¼" x 42"

Finished quilt size: 72" x 84" ■ Finished block size: 12" square

Pieced and machine quilted by Sheila Sinclair Snyder.

From the light background print #2, cut:

2 strips, 7¼" x 42"; crosscut into 9 squares, 7¼" x 7¼". Cut twice diagonally to make 36 quarter-square triangles.

5 strips, 3⅞" x 42"; crosscut into 44 squares, 3⅞" x 3⅞". Cut once diagonally to make 88 half-square triangles.

2 squares, 6⅞" x 6⅞"; cut once diagonally to make 4 half-square triangles.

MAKING THE BLOCKS

You need three different types of blocks to construct this quilt: 20 Time and Tide blocks, 18 side border blocks, and four corner border blocks.

Time and Tide Blocks

These blocks are constructed in units and set together in a nine-patch configuration. Templates are used for four components of the block. Use the patterns on page 27 to make templates for pieces A–D, being sure to include the seam lines.

1. Draw a diagonal line on the wrong side of each 5¼" purple square. Place a marked square right sides together with each 5¼" multicolored square. Sew ¼" from each side of the drawn line. Cut on the drawn line; press. Make 20 triangle-square units.

Make 20.

2. Draw a diagonal line on the wrong side of 10 units from step 1. Place a marked unit right sides together with an unmarked unit, with the purple triangle on top of the multicolored triangle. Butt the seam allowances. Sew ¼" from each side of the drawn line. Cut on the drawn line; press the seams in one direction. Make 20.

Make 20.

3. Place template B on a 4¾"-wide background print #1 strip, aligning one short side of the template with the cut edge of the strip as shown. Place a ruler over the template to cut one remaining side at a time. Cut 80.

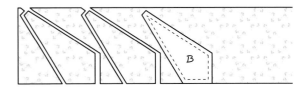

4. Use template A to trim the sharp points from each green A and A reverse triangle.

5. Using the marked seam allowances on the templates as a guide, sew an A triangle to one side of each B piece as shown; press. Sew an A reverse triangle to the adjacent side of each B piece; press. Square up the unit to 4½" x 4½". Make 80.

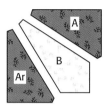

Make 80.

6. Place template D on a 4¾"-wide purple strip, aligning the base of the triangle with the cut edge of the strip as shown. Place a ruler over the template to cut one remaining side at a time. Reposition the template as shown, and cut the next triangle. Cut 40.

Cut 40 purple D triangles and 40 multicolored D triangles.

7. Repeat step 6 to cut 40 D triangles from the 4¾"-wide multicolored strips.

8. Use template C to trim the sharp point from each C and C reverse triangle.

9. Using the marked seam allowances on the templates as a guide, sew a C triangle to one side of each purple D triangle; press. Sew a C reverse triangle to the adjacent side of each D triangle; press. Square up the unit to 4½" x 4½". Make 40.

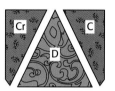

Make 40.

10. Repeat step 9 to sew a C and C reverse triangle to each multicolored D triangle; press. Make 40.

Make 40.

11. Arrange one unit from step 2, four units from step 5, and two units each from steps 9 and 10 in rows as shown. Sew the units into rows; press. Sew the rows together; press. Make 20 blocks.

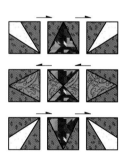 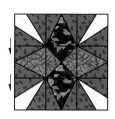

Make 20.

Side Border Blocks

1. Sew a 7¼" background print #2 quarter-square triangle to a 4¾" purple square as shown; press. Sew a 3⅞" background print #2 half-square triangle to the opposite side of the square as shown; press. Make 18.

Make 18.

2. Sew a 3⅞" background print #2 half-square triangle to the lower edge of each unit from step 1; press. Make 18.

Make 18.

3. Repeat steps 1 and 2 using the 4¾" multicolored squares in place of the purple squares. Make 18.

Make 18.

4. Sew a unit from step 2 to a unit from step 3 as shown; press. Make 18.

Make 18.

5. Sew a 3½" x 12½" green strip to opposite long sides of a unit from step 4 as shown. Do not press; you will press the seam allowances when you assemble the quilt. Make 18 blocks.

Make 18.

Corner Border Blocks

1. Sew a 4¾" multicolored square and a 4¾" purple square together as shown; press. Sew a 6⅞" background print #2 half-square triangle to the unit as shown, noting the placement of the colored squares; press. Make four.

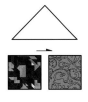

Make 4.

2. Sew two 3⅞" background print #2 half-square triangles to each 3½" green square to make a triangle unit as shown; press. Make four.

Make 4.

3. Sew a unit from step 2 to each unit from step 1 as shown; press. Sew two 3⅞" background print #2 half-square triangles to opposite ends of the unit as shown; press. Make four.

Make 4.

4. Sew a 3½" x 9½" green strip to the top edge of a unit from step 3 as shown; press. Sew a 3½" x 12½" green strip to the left side of the unit as shown; press. Make four blocks.

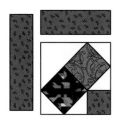
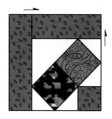

Make 4.

ASSEMBLING THE QUILT

1. Arrange the blocks in seven rows of six blocks each, referring to the quilt plan below for guidance. Once you've positioned the border blocks, press the seams in the top and bottom rows as shown.

2. Sew the blocks together into rows. Press the seams in opposite directions from row to row, including the seams within the remaining border blocks.

3. Sew the rows together; press.

FINISHING THE QUILT

1. Divide the backing fabric crosswise into two equal pieces. Remove the selvage and sew the pieces together to make a single backing piece with a vertical seam.

2. Layer the quilt top, batting, and backing; baste. (Professional machine quilters prefer to receive the quilt unbasted.)

3. Quilt as desired by hand or machine. I quilted an allover trailing leaf design in the center of the quilt, a geometric pattern in the light background, and a separate motif of trailing leaves for the border treatment.

4. Referring to pages 77–78 of "Tips and Techniques," use the 2¼"-wide green strips to bind your quilt.

5. Add a hanging sleeve and a label as described on pages 78–79.

Quilt Plan

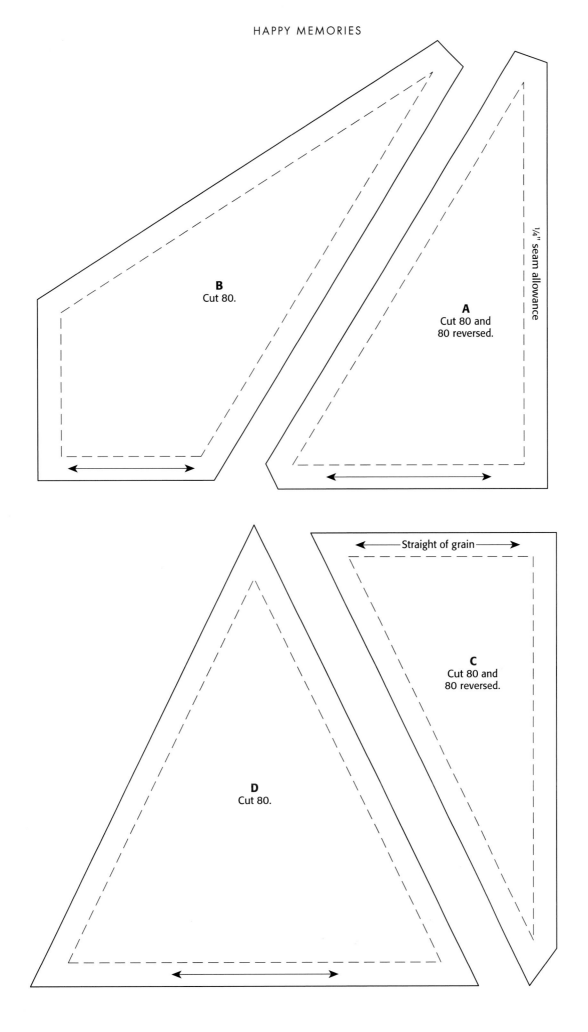

B
Cut 80.

A
Cut 80 and
80 reversed.

¼" seam allowance

Straight of grain

C
Cut 80 and
80 reversed.

D
Cut 80.

GEMSTONE MOSAIC

The rich hues of garnet, ruby, jade, and topaz give this quilt its elegance. The faceted look of the piecing is deceivingly simple. Pieced setting triangles surround four easy on-point blocks and are colored to give the illusion of a border. All combine to show off your piecing skills. Choose your favorite gemstone hues to complement your home decor. To create exciting contrast and simulate geologic forms, include a medium-light print—such as a bright, delicate floral—and a medium-dark print with black markings.

MATERIALS

Yardage amounts are based on 42"-wide fabrics.

- 2⅛ yards of medium-dark red print for blocks and setting triangles
- 1¾ yards of light topaz print for blocks and setting triangles
- 1¾ yards of medium-light red print for blocks, setting triangles, and binding
- 1⅛ yards of dark red print for blocks and setting triangles
- ⅞ yard of jade multicolored focus print for blocks and setting triangles
- 3½ yards of fabric for backing
- 63" x 77" piece of batting

CUTTING

All cutting instructions include ¼"-wide seam allowances.

From the light topaz print, cut:

10 strips, 3" x 42"

6 strips, 3⅜" x 42"; crosscut into 62 squares, 3⅜" x 3⅜". Cut once diagonally to make 124 half-square triangles.

4 squares, 4¼" x 4¼"; cut twice diagonally to make 16 quarter-square triangles

From the medium-dark red print, cut:

10 strips, 3" x 42"

4 strips, 2" x 42"; crosscut into 12 rectangles, 2" x 7⅝", and 12 rectangles, 2" x 4⅝"

2 strips, 3⅜" x 42"; crosscut into 12 squares, 3⅜" x 3⅜"

2 strips, 2⅝" x 42"; crosscut into 16 squares, 2⅝" x 2⅝"

4 strips, 1¾" x 42"

2 strips, 4⅞" x 42"; crosscut into 9 squares, 4⅞" x 4⅞"

Finished quilt size: 56½" × 70¾" ■ Finished block size: 10" square

Pieced and machine quilted by Sheila Sinclair Snyder.

From the dark red print, cut:

10 strips, 2" x 42"; crosscut into 26 rectangles, 2" x 7⅝"; 12 rectangles, 2" x 4⅝"; 28 rectangles, 2" x 2⅝"; 4 rectangles, 2" x 4"; and 4 rectangles, 2" x 2½"

2 strips, 3⅜" x 42"; crosscut into 12 squares, 3⅜" x 3⅜"

4 strips, 1¾" x 42"

From the jade multicolored focus print, cut:

2 strips, 4⅝" x 42"; crosscut into 12 squares, 4⅝" x 4⅝"

2 strips, 4" x 42"; crosscut into 16 squares, 4" x 4"

1 strip, 2⅝" x 42"; crosscut into 14 rectangles, 2⅝" x 4⅝"

4 squares, 2½" x 2½"

From the medium-light red print, cut:

3 strips, 3" x 42"; crosscut into 38 squares, 3" x 3"

2 strips, 2⅝" x 42"; crosscut into 16 squares, 2⅝" x 2⅝"

4 squares, 4¼" x 4¼"; cut twice diagonally to make 16 quarter-square triangles

2 strips, 4⅞" x 42"; crosscut into 9 squares, 4⅞" x 4⅞"

7 strips, 2¼" x 42"

MAKING THE BLOCKS

You need four different types of blocks to construct this quilt: 16 of block A, six each of blocks B and C, and four of block D.

Block A

1. Sew a 3"-wide topaz strip to a 3"-wide medium-dark red strip along one long edge; press. Make 10 strip sets.

Make 10 strip sets.

2. Sew strip sets from step 1 in pairs as shown. Make five strip sets. Cut the strip sets into 64 segments, 3" wide.

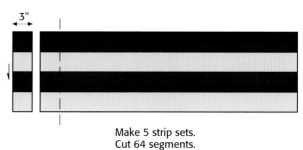

Make 5 strip sets.
Cut 64 segments.

3. Sew four segments from step 2 together as shown; press. Make 16 blocks.

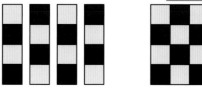

Block A
Make 16.

Block B

1. Sew a 2" x 4⅝" dark red rectangle to opposite sides of a 4⅝" jade square; press. Sew a 2" x 7⅝" dark red rectangle to the remaining sides of the square; press. Make six.

Make 6.

2. Sew a 3⅜" topaz half-square triangle to one side of a 3" medium-light red square; press. Sew a 3⅜" topaz half-square triangle to the adjacent side of the square as shown; press. Make 24.

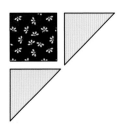 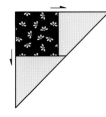

Make 24.

3. Sew a unit from step 2 to opposite sides of each unit from step 1 as shown; press. Sew a unit from step 2 to the remaining sides of each unit; press. Make six blocks.

Block B
Make 6.

Block C

1. Sew a 2" x 4⅝" medium-dark red rectangle to opposite sides of each remaining 4⅝" jade square; press. Sew a 2" x 7⅝" medium-dark red rectangle to the remaining sides of each square; press. Make six.

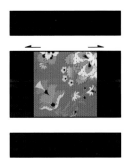 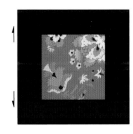

Make 6.

2. Draw a diagonal line on the wrong side of each 3⅜" medium-dark red square. Place a marked square right sides together with each 3⅜" dark red square. Sew ¼" from each side of the drawn line. Cut on the drawn line; press. Make 24 triangle-square units.

 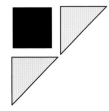

Make 24.

3. Sew a 3⅜" topaz half-square triangle to a dark edge of each unit from step 2 as shown; press. Sew a 3⅜" topaz half-square triangle to the adjacent dark edge of the unit; press. Make 24.

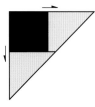

Make 24.

4. Sew a unit from step 3 to opposite sides of each unit from step 1; press. Sew a unit from step 3 to the remaining sides of the unit; press. Make six blocks.

Block C
Make 6.

Block D

This block will be slightly oversized; you will trim it to size when the block is complete.

1. Draw a diagonal line on the wrong side of each 2⅝" medium-dark red and 2⅝" medium-light red square.

2. Place a marked medium-dark red square right sides together with one corner of a 4" jade square. Stitch on the drawn line. Trim the excess seam allowance to ¼"; press. Repeat to sew a marked medium-light red square to the opposite corner of the jade square; trim and press. Make 16.

Make 16.

3. Arrange and sew four units from step 2 to make a four-patch block as shown, carefully noting the placement of the medium-light and medium-dark red triangles; press. Make four.

  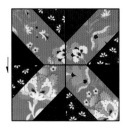

Make 4.

4. Sew the long edges of the 4¼" topaz quarter-square triangles to the 1¾"-wide medium-dark red strips, allowing 3" between triangles as shown; press. Align a small square ruler with the corner of the triangle and trim the strip to form a larger triangle as shown. Cut 16. Repeat, using the 4¼" medium-light red quarter-square triangles and the 1¾"-wide dark red strips, and pressing in the opposite direction. Cut 16.

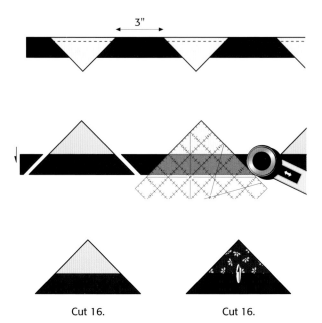

Cut 16. Cut 16.

5. Sew two triangle units from step 4, one of each color combination, together as shown, noting the placement of the colors and matching the seam lines; press. Make 16.

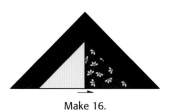

Make 16.

6. Sew a unit from step 5 to opposite sides of each unit from step 3; press. Sew a unit from step 5 to the remaining sides of the unit; press. Square up the block to 10½" x 10½". Make four blocks.

Block D
Make 4.

MAKING THE SETTING TRIANGLES

You need two different types of pieced setting triangles: 14 of triangle E (side setting triangles), and four of triangle F (corner setting triangles).

Triangle E

1. Sew a 2" x 2⅝" dark red rectangle to each short edge of a 2⅝" x 4⅝" jade rectangle as shown; press. Sew a 2" x 7⅝" dark red rectangle to one long edge of each unit as shown; press. Make 14.

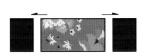

Make 14.

2. Sew two 3⅜" topaz half-square triangles to a 3" medium-light red square; press. Make 14.

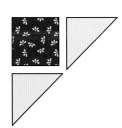

Make 14.

3. Sew a triangle unit from step 2 to each unit from step 1 as shown; press. Make 14.

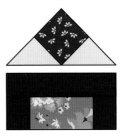

Make 14.

4. Draw a diagonal line on the wrong side of seven of the 4⅞" medium-light red squares. Place a marked square right sides together with a 4⅞" medium-dark red square. Sew ¼" from each side of the drawn line. Cut on the drawn line; press. Make 14 triangle-square units.

Make 14.

5. Cut each unit from step 4 once diagonally as shown to make 28 triangles.

Cut 28 triangles.

6. Sew a triangle unit from step 5 to opposite ends of each unit from step 3 as shown; press. Make 14 side setting triangles.

Triangle E
Make 14.

33

Triangle F

1. Sew a 2" x 2½" dark red rectangle to one side of a 2½" jade square as shown; press. Sew a 2" x 4" dark red rectangle to each unit as shown; press. Make four.

Make 4.

2. Draw a diagonal line on the wrong side of the two remaining 4⅞" medium-light red squares. Place a marked square right sides together with a 4⅞" medium-dark red square. Sew ¼" from each side of the drawn line. Cut on the drawn line; press. Make four triangle-square units.

Make 4.

3. Cut each unit from step 2 once diagonally as shown to make eight triangles.

Cut 8 triangles.

4. Sew two triangle units from step 3 to each unit from step 1 as shown; press. Make four corner setting triangles.

Triangle F
Make 4.

ASSEMBLING THE QUILT

1. Arrange the blocks, side setting triangles, and corner setting triangles in diagonal rows, referring to the photo on page 29 and the assembly diagram below for guidance.

Assembly Diagram

2. Sew the blocks into rows. Press the seams in opposite directions from row to row.

3. Sew the rows together. Press the seams in one direction.

4. Sew the corner triangles to the quilt. Press the seams away from the triangles.

FINISHING THE QUILT

1. Divide the backing fabric crosswise into two equal pieces. Remove the selvage and sew the pieces together to make a single backing piece with a horizontal seam.

2. Layer the quilt top, batting, and backing; baste. (Professional machine quilters prefer to receive the quilt unbasted.)

3. Quilt as desired by hand or machine. I chose a flowing, curvy, allover design to balance the geometry of this quilt.

4. Referring to pages 77–78 of "Tips and Techniques," use the 2¼"-wide medium-light red strips to bind your quilt.

5. Add a hanging sleeve and a label as described on pages 78–79.

Quilt Plan

PARTY ATTITUDE

Think fiesta, birthdays, the Fourth of July, and New Year's Eve! Now, let those images inspire you to select the fabrics for this quilt. It will definitely put you in a party mood. See how easy it is to complete this quilt when all the components are made first!

MATERIALS

Yardage amounts are based on 42"-wide fabric.

- 6⅞ yards *total* of assorted light pink prints for blocks
- 2¼ yards *total* of assorted vibrant pink and related-color prints for blocks
- 7½ yards of fabric for backing
- ¾ yard of pink fabric for binding
- 90" x 102" piece of batting

CUTTING

All cutting instructions include ¼"-wide seam allowances.

From the assorted light pink prints, cut a *total* of:

56 strips, 3½" x 42"; crosscut 14 strips into 144 squares, 3½" x 3½". Set the remaining strips aside.

11 strips, 3⅞" x 42"; crosscut into 106 squares, 3⅞" x 3⅞"

From the assorted vibrant pink and related-color prints, cut a *total* of:

8 strips, 3½" x 42"; crosscut into 84 squares, 3½" x 3½"

11 strips, 3⅞" x 42"; crosscut into 106 squares, 3⅞" x 3⅞"

From the pink fabric for binding, cut:

10 strips, 2¼" x 42"

MAKING THE BLOCKS

You need eight different types of blocks to construct this quilt: 12 plain blocks (block A), eight Star blocks (block B), eight pieced half-square-triangle blocks (block C), two pieced quarter-square-triangle blocks (block D), four corner border blocks (block E), 10 side border blocks (block F), 10 reverse side border blocks (block G), and two center border blocks (block H).

You need only two shapes (a square and a half-square triangle) to make up each of these blocks. The shapes are assembled into units in advance to make the most efficient use of your fabric and your time. Working this way also allows for a variety of fabric combinations and a great scrappy look.

Unit 1 and Unit 2

1. Sew two different 3½"-wide light pink strips together along one long edge; press. Make 21 strip sets, randomly combining fabrics. Cut the strip sets into 228 segments, 3½" wide, and label them unit 1.

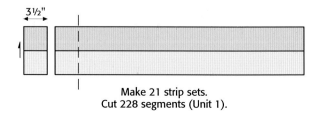

Make 21 strip sets.
Cut 228 segments (Unit 1).

Finished quilt size: 84" × 96" ■ Finished block size: 12" square

Pieced by Yolaine Adams, Sally Franzoni, and Sheila Sinclair Snyder.
Machine quilted by Sheila Sinclair Snyder.

2. Draw a diagonal line on the wrong side of each 3⅞" light pink square. Place a marked square right sides together with a 3⅞" vibrant pink square. Sew ¼" from each side of the drawn line. Cut on the drawn line; press. Make 212 triangle-square units and label them unit 2.

Unit 2
Make 212.

You now have all of the components you need to construct the blocks for this quilt.

Block A

1. Arrange eight unit 1 segments to make a 16-patch block. Make adjustments for fabric variety and scrappy effect as needed.

2. Sew the units into rows; press.

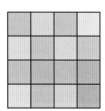

3. Sew the rows together. Do not press; you will press the seams later. Make 12 blocks.

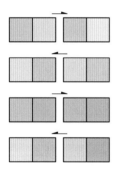

Block A
Make 12.

Block B

1. Arrange four 3½" light pink squares, four 3½" vibrant pink squares, and eight of unit 2 as shown below.

2. Sew the units into rows; press.

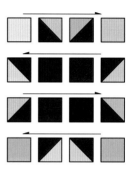

3. Sew the rows together. Do not press; you will press the seams later. Make eight blocks.

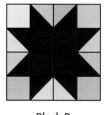

Block B
Make 8.

Block C

1. Arrange two unit 1 segments, four of unit 2, two 3½" light pink squares, and six 3½" vibrant pink squares as shown below.

2. Sew the units into rows; press.

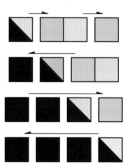

3. Sew the rows together. Do not press; you will press the seams later. Make eight blocks.

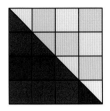

Block C
Make 8.

Block D

1. Arrange four unit 1 segments, four of unit 2, two 3½" light pink squares, and two 3½" vibrant pink squares as shown below.

2. Sew the units into rows; press.

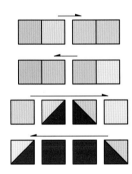

3. Sew the rows together. Do not press; you will press the seams later. Make two blocks.

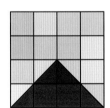

Block D
Make 2.

Block E

1. Arrange four unit 1 segments, five of unit 2, and three 3½" light pink squares as shown at upper right.

2. Sew the units into rows; press.

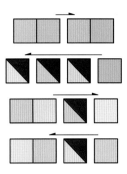

3. Sew the rows together. Do not press; you will press the seams later. Make four blocks.

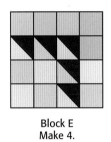

Block E
Make 4.

Block F

1. Arrange four unit 1 segments, four of unit 2, and four 3½" light pink squares as shown below.

2. Sew the units into rows; press.

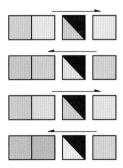

3. Sew the rows together. Do not press; you will press the seams later. Make 10 blocks.

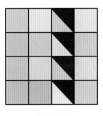

Block F
Make 10.

Block G

1. Arrange four unit 1 segments, four of unit 2, and four 3½" light pink squares as shown below.

2. Sew the units into rows; press.

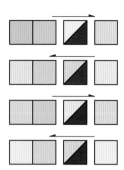

3. Sew the rows together. Do not press; you will press the seams later. Make 10 blocks.

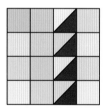

Block G
Make 10.

Block H

1. Arrange six unit 1 segments and four of unit 2 as shown below.

2. Sew the units into rows; press.

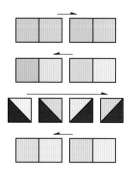

3. Sew the rows together. Do not press; you will press the seams later. Make two blocks.

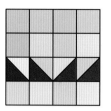

Block H
Make 2.

ASSEMBLING THE QUILT

1. Arrange the blocks in eight rows of seven blocks each, referring to the quilt plan on page 41 for guidance. Audition blocks in different locations as needed to get the best balance of color. Pay particular attention to the orientation of the dark triangles in the border blocks.

2. Sew the blocks into rows, pressing the seams of each block as you go. Alternate pressing the seam allowances up for one block and down for the next. When you've finished the rows, press the seams in opposite directions from row to row.

DESIGNER'S TIP
Some of the seam allowances you've already pressed may not dovetail with the next block as you expect. Don't worry: these seams are limited in number and the fabrics are light-weight enough that you can press the intersections adequately and keep bulk to a minimum.

3. Sew the rows together; press.

FINISHING THE QUILT

1. Divide the backing fabric crosswise into three equal pieces. Remove the selvage and sew the pieces together to make a single backing piece with two horizontal seams.

2. Layer the quilt top, batting, and backing; baste. (Professional machine quilters prefer to receive the quilt unbasted.)

3. Quilt as desired by hand or machine. I quilted this quilt with an allover ribbon design.

4. Referring to pages 77–78 of "Tips and Techniques," use the 2¼"-wide pink strips to bind your quilt.

5. Add a hanging sleeve and a label as described on pages 78–79.

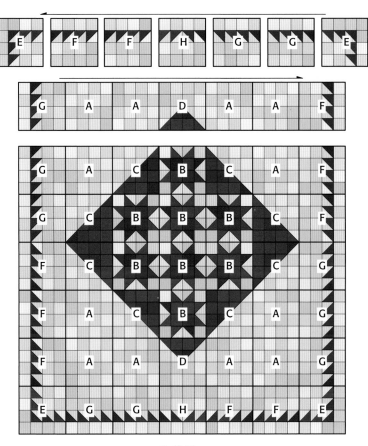

Quilt Plan

ADJUST THE HORIZONTAL

The zigzag motion of this quilt puts me in mind of the test patterns we watched as children on Saturday mornings while we waited for the cartoons to begin. That eerie tone, those black-and-white designs, and the anticipation of the upcoming animated delights may have been the start of my appreciation for color: dreaming of the possibilities beyond gray scale!

MATERIALS

Yardage amounts are based on 42"-wide fabric.

- 1⅛ yards of black solid for blocks
- 1⅛ yards of large-scale focus print for blocks
- 1 yard of green dotted print for blocks
- 1 yard of multicolored speckled print for blocks
- 3½ yards of fabric for backing
- ½ yard of black print for binding
- 56" x 56" piece of batting

CUTTING

All cutting instructions include ¼"-wide seam allowances.

From the large-scale focus print, cut:
2 strips, 9¼" x 42"; crosscut into 8 squares, 9¼" x 9¼". Cut twice diagonally to make 32 quarter-square triangles.

3 strips, 5¼" x 42"; crosscut into 18 squares, 5¼" x 5¼". Cut twice diagonally to make 72 quarter-square triangles.

From the black solid, cut:
2 strips, 9¼" x 42"; crosscut into 8 squares, 9¼" x 9¼". Cut twice diagonally to make 32 quarter-square triangles.

3 strips, 5¼" x 42"; crosscut into 18 squares, 5¼" x 5¼". Cut twice diagonally to make 72 quarter-square triangles.

From the green dotted print, cut:
2 strips, 6½" x 42
2 strips, 2" x 42"
3 strips, 3½" x 42"
3 strips, 1¼" x 42"

From the multicolored speckled print, cut:
2 strips, 2" x 42"
2 strips, 6½" x 42"
3 strips, 1¼" x 42"
3 strips, 3½" x 42"

From the black print, cut:
6 strips, 2¼" x 42"

Finished quilt size: 50" × 50" ■ Finished block sizes: 10" square (Block A); 5" square (Block B)

Pieced and machine quilted by Sheila Sinclair Snyder.

MAKING THE BLOCKS

You need two different types of blocks to construct this quilt: 16 of block A and 36 of block B. Block B will be used to create three different units for the border.

Block A

1. Sew a large focus-print triangle and a large black triangle together as shown; press. Make 32.

Make 32.

2. Sew a 6½"-wide green strip, a 2"-wide speckled strip, a 2"-wide green strip, and a 6½"-wide speckled strip along the long edges in the order shown; press. Make two strip sets. Crosscut the strip sets into 32 segments, 2" wide.

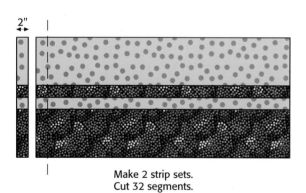

Make 2 strip sets.
Cut 32 segments.

3. Sew two segments from step 2 together as shown. Press the center seam open to reduce the bulk in subsequent steps. Make 16.

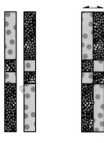

Make 16.

4. Sew a unit from step 1 to opposite long sides of each unit from step 3 as shown, matching the center seam line; press. (The center unit will extend beyond the triangles.) Make 16.

Make 16.

5. Square up the blocks to 10½" x 10½", carefully matching the 45° mark on your ruler with the center diagonal seam of the block as shown.

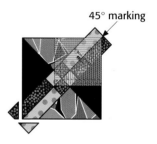

45° marking

Block B

Block B is constructed in the same fashion as Block A. Refer to the illustrations at left and above as needed.

1. Sew a small focus-print triangle and a small black triangle together; press. Make 72.

2. Sew a 3½"-wide green strip, a 1¼"-wide speckled strip, a 1¼"-wide green strip, and a 3½"-wide speckled strip along the long edges in the order listed; press. Make three strip sets. Crosscut the strip sets into 72 segments, 1¼" wide.

3. Sew two segments from step 2 together. Press the center seam open to reduce bulk in subsequent steps. Make 36.

4. Sew a unit from step 1 to opposite long sides of each unit from step 3, matching the center seam line; press. (The center unit will extend beyond the triangles.) Make 36.

5. Square up the blocks to 5½" x 5½", carefully matching the 45° mark on your ruler with the center diagonal seam of the block.

ASSEMBLING THE BORDER UNITS

1. Sew two B blocks together with the pieced diagonal strips forming a V as shown; press. Make 16 and label them border unit B1.

Border Unit B1
Make 16.

2. Sew a B block to the right edge of a border unit B1; press. Make two and label them border unit B2.

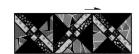

Border Unit B2
Make 2.

3. Sew a B block to the left edge of a border unit B1; press. Make two and label them border unit B3.

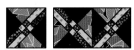

Border Unit B3
Make 2.

ASSEMBLING THE QUILT

1. Arrange the A blocks and border units B1–B3, referring to the photo on page 43 and the assembly diagram below for guidance. Carefully turn each block and border unit as shown.

2. Sew a border unit B1 to the top edge of each block in the top row; press. Repeat to sew a border unit B1 to the bottom edge of each block in the bottom row; press.

Assembly Diagram

3. Sew the blocks and remaining border units together into rows. Press the seams in opposite directions from row to row.

4. Sew the rows together; press.

FINISHING THE QUILT

1. Divide the backing fabric crosswise into two equal pieces. Remove the selvage and sew the pieces together to make a single backing piece with a vertical seam.

2. Layer the quilt top, batting, and backing; baste. (Professional machine quilters prefer to receive the quilt unbasted.) I chose black batting for this quilt to prevent any light-colored batting from whiskering through the fabric or the quilting stitches.

3. Quilt as desired by hand or machine. I created an allover swirl design on this quilt.

4. Referring to pages 77–78 of "Tips and Techniques," use the 2¼"-wide black print strips to bind your quilt.

5. Add a hanging sleeve and a label as described on pages 78–79.

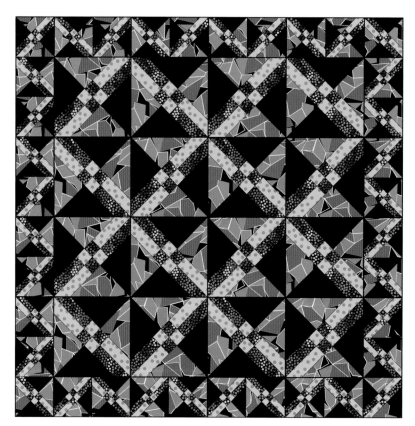

Quilt Plan

HIGHLY HUGGABLE

Soft pastel flannels come to life in this cozy quilt! I recommend 15 to 20—or even more—different pastel prints to yield enough variety for a scrappy effect. Choose a mix of florals, plaids, stripes, checks, and other prints in the light to medium range. For best results, select a tightly woven solid in a light value for the block backgrounds.

MATERIALS

Yardage amounts are based on 42"-wide fabric.

- 3 yards *total* of 15 to 20 assorted pastel prints for blocks and sashing*
- ⅞ yard of light solid for block backgrounds
- 3 yards of pastel print for backing
- ½ yard of light pastel print for binding
- 51" x 66" piece of batting

Fat quarters (18" x 22") are a good choice, as well as scraps approximately 10" x 10".

CUTTING

All cutting instructions include ¼"-wide seam allowances.

From *each* of 12 assorted pastel prints, cut:
4 rectangles, 2¾" x 3½" (48 total)
1 square, 5½" x 5½" (12 total)

From the assorted pastel prints, cut a *total* of:
48 squares, 3⅞" x 3⅞"; cut once diagonally to make 96 half-square triangles
144 squares, 3½" x 3½"

From the light solid, cut:
3 strips, 5½" x 42"; crosscut into 48 rectangles, 2½" x 5½"

3 strips, 2½" x 42"; crosscut into 48 squares, 2½" x 2½"

From the light pastel print for binding, cut:
6 strips, 2¼" x 42"

MAKING THE BLOCKS

You need 12 Star blocks to construct this quilt. You will piece the star points as flying-geese units. I modified the construction of the units to avoid bulk at the seam intersections in subsequent steps. Because I used flannel for my quilt, I further reduced bulk by pressing the seams open. If you are not using flannel, press the seams toward the darker fabrics.

1. Sort the 2¾" x 3½" pastel rectangles into two stacks of 24 rectangles each, with each stack containing two rectangles of the same fabric.

Finished quilt size: 45" × 60" ▪ Finished block size: 15" square (includes sashing)

Pieced and machine quilted by Sheila Sinclair Snyder.

2. Cut the rectangles in one stack once diagonally to make 48 triangles. Cut the rectangles in the remaining stack once diagonally *in the opposite direction* to make 48 triangles. Turn the triangles over and use a water-soluble pen to mark the ¼" seam allowance along the diagonally cut edge of each triangle as shown. Label the stacks L (for left) and R (for right).

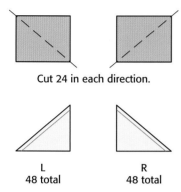

Cut 24 in each direction.

L
48 total

R
48 total

3. Use a water-soluble pen to make a dot at the midpoint of one long side of each 2½" x 5½" light rectangle, ¼" from the cut edge as shown. You will use this marking to accurately position the star points for sewing.

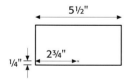

5½"

2¾"

¼"

DESIGNER'S TIP
To speed assembly of these blocks, you may wish to try a technique called chain piecing. See pages 75–76 of "Tips and Techniques" for details.

4. Place an R triangle right sides together with each 2½" x 5½" light rectangle as shown. Use the marked seam line on the diagonal cut edge of the triangle and the dot on the rectangle for placement as shown; pin. Sew the triangle to the rectangle with a ¼" seam.

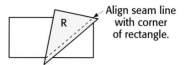

R

Align seam line with corner of rectangle.

5. Trim away the excess light fabric, leaving a ¼"-wide seam allowance. Press the seam open and trim the "dog ears" to eliminate bulk and help keep your quilt top flat. Make 48.

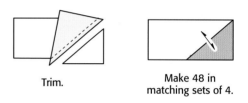

Trim.

Make 48 in matching sets of 4.

6. Repeat steps 4 and 5 to sew a matching L triangle to each unit as shown; trim and press. You will have 48 flying-geese units in matching sets of four. The units should measure 2½" x 5½".

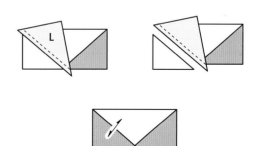

L

Make 48 in matching sets of 4.

7. Arrange four 2½" light squares, one 5½" pastel square, and four matching flying-geese units from step 6 as shown. Sew the units and squares into rows. Press the seams open. Sew the rows together. Press the seams open. Square up the block to 9½" x 9½". Make 12 blocks.

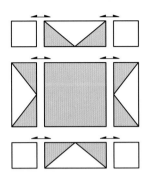 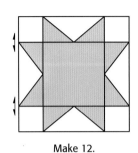

Make 12.

ADDING THE SASHING

1. Sew three 3½" pastel print squares in a row as shown, mixing and matching colors. Press the seams open. Make 48.

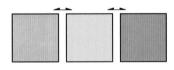

Make 48.

2. Sew assorted pastel half-square triangles together in pairs along the long bias edges, mixing and matching for a scrappy effect. Press the seams open. (Be careful not to stretch the bias!) Make 48.

Make 48.

DESIGNER'S NOTE
While you may know other shortcut methods for creating triangle-square units, making them individually will give you the scrappiest effect.

3. Sew a unit from step 2 to each end of a unit from step 1 as shown. Press the seams open. Make 24.

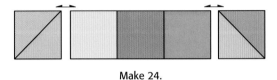

Make 24.

4. Arrange a Star block, two units from step 1, and two units from step 3 as shown. Sew the block and units together into rows. Press the seams open. Sew the rows together. Press the seams open. Square up the block to 15½" x 15½". Make 12 blocks.

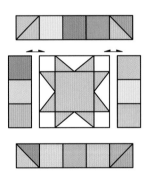 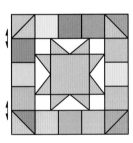

Make 12.

ASSEMBLING THE QUILT

1. Arrange the blocks in four rows of three blocks each, referring to the quilt plan below for guidance.

2. Sew the blocks together into rows. Press the seams in opposite directions from row to row.

3. Sew the rows together; press.

FINISHING THE QUILT

1. Divide the backing fabric crosswise into two equal pieces. Remove the selvage and sew the pieces together to make a single backing piece with a horizontal seam.

2. Layer the quilt top, batting, and backing; baste. (Professional machine quilters prefer to receive the quilt unbasted.)

3. Quilt as desired by hand or machine. On flannel quilts, my preference is for simple quilting such as meandering, allover swirls, or simple designs from nature.

4. Referring to pages 77–78 of "Tips and Techniques," use the 2¼"-wide light pastel print strips to bind your quilt.

5. Add a hanging sleeve and a label as described on pages 78–79.

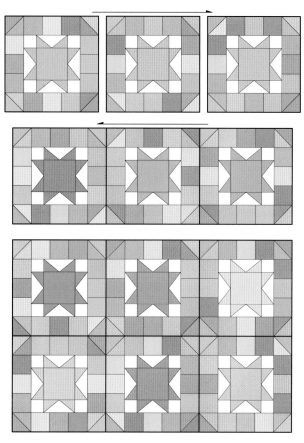

Quilt Plan

TARZAN IN NEW YORK

The golds and earthy animal-print fabrics in this quilt are jazzed up with the juxtaposition of sophisticated, hand-dyed cottons in green, red, olive, and brown. The feeling is uptown, wild, pulsating, and mesmerizing. It's such a tangle of color, you just can't take your eyes away. The finishing touch is a pieced border, attached in a unique way to make the quilt construction simple and the results accurate. I chose not to include a top border primarily to control the size and shape of the quilt. I felt the fabrics and design were strong enough to finish the quilt as it is.

MATERIALS

Yardage amounts are based on 42"-wide fabric.

- 2¾ yards *total* of assorted medium-dark and dark prints for sashing
- 2½ yards *total* of assorted light prints for sashing
- 2⅛ yards of red hand-dyed fabric for Pinwheel A and B blocks
- 1⅛ yards of animal print #1 for Pinwheel A blocks
- 1⅛ yards of green hand-dyed fabric for Pinwheel B blocks
- 1⅛ yards *total* of assorted yellow prints for sashing squares
- 1⅛ yards of brown hand-dyed fabric for border blocks
- ¾ yard of olive green hand-dyed fabric for border blocks
- ¾ yard of animal print #2 for border blocks
- 9 yards of fabric for backing
- ¾ yard of dark small-scale animal print for binding
- 102" x 108" piece of batting

DESIGNER'S TIP

The one-of-a-kind hand-dyed fabrics used in this quilt were purchased from Jeanette Viviano of Portland, Oregon. She also overdyed a zebra-stripe fabric from my collection to match the color scheme of this quilt. See more of her creations at www.jeanettesfabrictodyefor.com.

CUTTING

All cutting instructions include ¼"-wide seam allowances.

From the animal print #1, cut:
7 strips, 4⅞" x 42"; crosscut into 56 squares, 4⅞" x 4⅞"

From the red hand-dyed fabric, cut:
14 strips, 4⅞" x 42"; crosscut into 112 squares, 4⅞" x 4⅞"

From the green hand-dyed fabric, cut:
7 strips, 4⅞" x 42"; crosscut into 56 squares, 4⅞" x 4⅞"

Finished quilt size: 96" x 102" ■ Finished block sizes: 12" square
(Pinwheel blocks, including sashing); 6" square (border blocks)

Pieced and machine quilted by Sheila Sinclair Snyder.

From the assorted light prints, cut a *total* of:

16 strips, 5¼" x 42"; crosscut into 112 squares, 5¼" x 5¼". Cut twice diagonally to make 448 quarter-square triangles.

From the assorted medium-dark and dark prints, cut a *total* of:

8 strips, 5¼" x 42"; crosscut into 56 squares, 5¼" x 5¼". Cut twice diagonally to make 224 quarter-square triangles.

18 strips, 2⅞" x 42"; crosscut into 224 squares, 2⅞" x 2⅞". Cut once diagonally to make 448 half-square triangles.

From the assorted yellow prints, cut a *total* of:

14 strips, 2½" x 42"; crosscut into 224 squares, 2½" x 2½"

From the olive green hand-dyed fabric, cut:

3 strips, 7¼" x 42"; crosscut into 12 squares, 7¼" x 7¼". Cut twice diagonally to make 48 quarter-square triangles.

From the animal print #2, cut:

3 strips, 7¼" x 42"; crosscut into 12 squares, 7¼" x 7¼". Cut twice diagonally to make 48 quarter-square triangles.

From the brown hand-dyed fabric, cut:

5 strips, 7¼" x 42"; crosscut into 24 squares, 7¼" x 7¼". Cut twice diagonally to make 96 quarter-square triangles.

From the small-scale animal print, cut:

11 strips, 2¼" x 42"

DESIGNER'S TIP

I fussy cut the animal print #2 squares so that the eyes of the big cat would appear to look out from the quilt.

Detail of Border Block

MAKING THE BLOCKS

You need three different types of blocks to construct this quilt: 28 each of Pinwheel A and B and 48 border blocks.

Pinwheel A and B Blocks

1. Draw a diagonal line on the wrong side of each 4⅞" animal print #1 square. Place a marked square right sides together with a 4⅞" red square. Sew ¼" from each side of the drawn line. Cut on the drawn line; press. Make 112 triangle-square units.

Make 112.

2. Arrange and sew four units from step 1 as shown; press. Make 28 blocks and label them Pinwheel A.

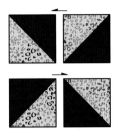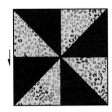

Pinwheel A
Make 28.

3. Repeat steps 1 and 2 using the 4⅞" green squares and the remaining 4⅞" red squares. Make 28 blocks and label them Pinwheel B.

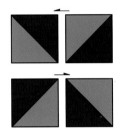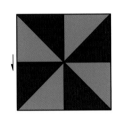

Pinwheel B
Make 28.

ADDING THE SASHING

1. Separate the light quarter-square triangles into two stacks of 224 triangles each. You may have multiples of the same fabric within a stack, but identical fabrics should not appear in both stacks. Label the stacks A and B.

2. Repeat step 1 to separate the large medium-dark and dark (quarter-square) triangles into two stacks (A and B) of 112 triangles each.

3. Repeat step 1 to separate the small medium-dark and dark (half-square) triangles into two stacks (A and B) of 224 triangles each.

4. Repeat step 1 to separate the 2½" yellow squares into two stacks (A and B) of 112 squares each.

5. Starting with the A stacks, arrange two light triangles from step 1, one medium-dark or dark triangle from step 2, and two medium-dark or dark triangles from step 3 as shown. Sew the small dark triangles to the adjacent light triangle first; press. Sew these units to the opposite sides of the large dark triangle; press. Make 112, with the fabric combinations as random as possible.

Sashing Unit A
Make 112.

6. Sew a 2½" yellow square to each end of a randomly selected unit from step 5 as shown; press. Make 56.

Make 56 with sashing squares.

DESIGNER'S TIP

If you wish, cut an extra piece of each shape, mark the seam lines, sew the seams, and use this sample as a template for putting the sashing units together. Doing so will increase your accuracy and save time in construction. I sometimes tape the sample to my worktable or sewing machine so I can check each piece as I sew the block or unit together.

7. Arrange a Pinwheel A block, two sashing units from step 5, and two sashing units from step 6 as shown. Sew the block and units together; press. Make 28 blocks.

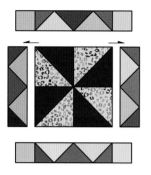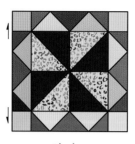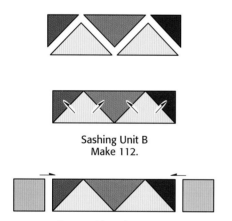

Block A
Make 28.

8. Repeat steps 5 and 6 to assemble the sashing units for Pinwheel B. Use the triangles and squares from the B stacks, and press as shown. Make 112 units total. Sew 2½" yellow squares to each end of 56 units.

Sashing Unit B
Make 112.

Make 56 with sashing squares.

9. Arrange and sew a Pinwheel B block and two of each type of sashing unit from step 8 as shown; press. Square up the block to 12½" x 12½". Make 28 blocks.

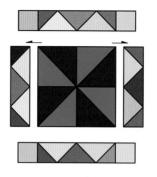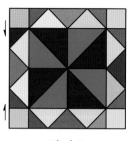

Block B
Make 28.

BORDER BLOCKS

1. Sew each olive green triangle to a brown triangle as shown; press. Repeat to sew each animal print #2 triangle to a brown triangle; press. Make 48 of each.

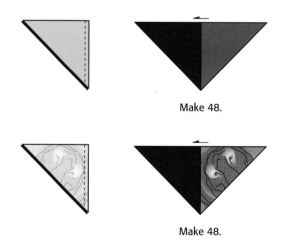

Make 48.

Make 48.

2. Sew each olive/brown unit to an animal print/brown unit, matching the center seam as shown. Press in one direction. Make 48.

Make 48.

3. Sew two units from step 2 together as shown; press. Make 21.

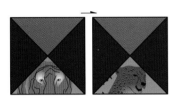

Make 21.

4. Sew three units from step 2 together as shown; press. Make two.

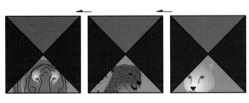

Make 2.

ASSEMBLING THE QUILT

1. Arrange the Pinwheel and border blocks in rows, referring to the photo on page 53 and the assembly diagram below for guidance. Alternate the Pinwheel A and B blocks as shown.

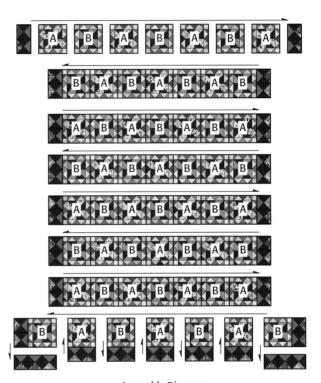

Assembly Diagram

2. Sew the border units to the blocks in the bottom row. Press as shown.

3. Sew the blocks and remaining border units together into rows. Press the seams in opposite directions from row to row.

4. Sew the rows together; press.

FINISHING THE QUILT

1. Divide the backing fabric crosswise into three equal pieces. Remove the selvage and sew the pieces together to make a single backing piece with two horizontal seams.

2. Layer the quilt top, batting, and backing; baste. (Professional machine quilters prefer to receive the quilt unbasted.)

3. Quilt as desired by hand or machine. I quilted an allover design of waves and swirls on this quilt.

4. Referring to pages 77–78 of "Tips and Techniques," use the 2¼"-wide animal print strips to bind your quilt.

5. Add a hanging sleeve and a label as described on pages 78–79.

Quilt Plan

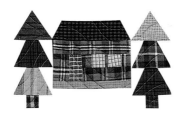

PONDEROSA RETREAT

How many of us have warm memories of a cabin in the woods? With this quilt, you can have your cabin in the middle of the city and cozy up every night. Round up all the homespun plaids, checks, and stripes in your stash, and then add to them from the wide variety available at your local quilt shop. Give the quilt that down-home feeling with the softness of muslin, and you've got a combination sure to give you a warm feeling in more ways than one! Fat quarters, fat eighths, and scraps all work well for this project and add to the scrappy effect.

MATERIALS

Yardage amounts are based on 42"-wide fabric.

- 2⅝ yards of unbleached muslin for background
- 1¾ yards *total* of homespuns in assorted colors for cabin siding, roofs, doors, and nine-patch units
- 1⅜ yards *total* of assorted green homespuns for cabin and tree units
- ¼ yard *total* of assorted brown and black homespuns for tree units
- ¼ yard *total* of assorted yellow and gold homespuns for cabin windows
- 3 yards of fabric for backing
- ½ yard of homespun for binding
- 54" x 66" piece of batting

CUTTING

All cutting instructions include ¼"-wide seam allowances.

From the unbleached muslin, cut:

4 strips, 2" x 42"; crosscut into 40 rectangles, 2" x 3"

1 strip, 6½" x 42"; crosscut into 40 strips, 1" x 6½"

9 strips, 2½" x 42"; crosscut into 160 rectangles, 1½" x 2½", and 40 squares, 2½" x 2½"

15 strips, 3½" x 42"; crosscut 4 strips into 40 rectangles, 2¼" x 3½", and 40 rectangles, 1½" x 3½". Set the remaining strips aside.

2 strips, 1½" x 42"

Finished quilt size: 48" × 60"　■　Finished block size: 12" square

Pieced and machine quilted by Sheila Sinclair Snyder.

From the homespuns in assorted colors, cut 20 matching sets* that each include:

1 rectangle, 1¾" x 2½"

1 strip, 1½" x 16"; crosscut into:

    1 rectangle, 1½" x 6½"

    1 rectangle, 1½" x 4¼"

    2 rectangles, 1¼" x 1½"

    1 rectangle, ¾" x 1½"

From the remaining homespuns in assorted colors, cut:

19 strips, 1½" x 40"; crosscut into 480 squares, 1½" x 1½"

20 rectangles, 2" x 6½"

20 rectangles, 1½" x 2½"

From the assorted green homespuns, cut a *total* of:

20 rectangles, 1" x 6½"

10 strips, 3½" x 42"

From the assorted yellow and gold homespuns, cut a *total* of:

40 squares, 1½" x 1½" (in matching pairs)

From the assorted brown and black homespuns, cut a *total* of:

40 squares, 1½" x 1½"

From the homespun for binding, cut:

6 strips, 2¼" x 42"

*Cut all rectangles from the same fabric to create a set.

CONSTRUCTING THE UNITS

You need 20 of a single block to construct this quilt. The block is constructed in units, and then set together in vertical rows.

Cabin Units

1. Draw a diagonal line through the center of each 2" x 3" muslin rectangle on the wrong side. Draw the line in one direction on 20 rectangles and in the opposite direction on the remaining 20 rectangles as shown. Keep the marked rectangles sorted into two separate stacks.

Mark 20 in each direction.

2. Position one muslin rectangle from each stack, marked side up, over a 2" x 6½" homespun rectangle, right side up. Position each muslin piece so that the drawn line extends ¼" beyond the top edge of the homespun rectangle, is 1" in from the top corner of the rectangle, and aligns perfectly with the lower corner of the rectangle as shown.

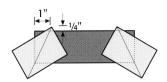

3. Sew on the drawn lines; press. Square up the unit to 2" x 6½" and trim the excess seam allowance to ¼". Make 20.

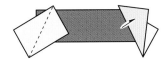

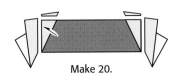

Make 20.

4. Using a matching set of homespun pieces, matching 1½" yellow squares, a unit from step 3, two 1" x 6½" muslin rectangles, a 1" x 6½" green rectangle, and a 1½" x 2½" homespun rectangle, assemble the cabin unit in sections as shown; press.

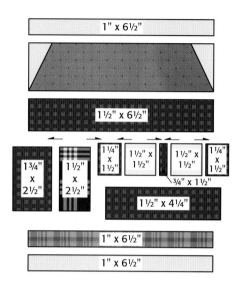

5. Sew the sections together into rows; press. Sew the rows together; press.

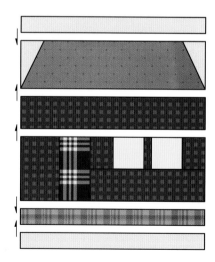

6. Square up the unit to 6½" x 6½".

7. Repeat steps 4–6 to make 20 cabin units.

Nine-Patch Units

The nine-patch design is revealed when the completed blocks are sewn together.

1. Sew 1½" homespun squares in assorted colors into random pairs; press. Make 200.

Make 200.

2. Sew units from step 1 into random four-patch units; press. Make 80.

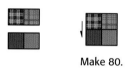

Make 80.

3. Arrange one unit from step 1, two units from step 2, two 1½" x 2½" muslin rectangles, and one 2½" muslin square as shown. Sew the units, rectangles, and squares together into rows. Make 40 of each row; press.

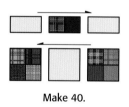

Make 40.

4. Sew the rows together; press.

5. Sew one unit from step 4 to the top and one to the bottom of each cabin unit as shown; press. Make 20.

Make 20.

Tree Units

The trees in these units are paper-pieced. Refer to pages 76–77 of "Tips and Techniques" as needed.

1. Use the pattern on page 65 to trace or copy 40 paper foundations for the tree units.

2. Construct the trees in numerical sequence. Use the 1½" brown or black squares for the tree trunks (piece 1), the 3½"-wide assorted green strips for the trees (pieces 4, 7, and 10), and the 1½"-wide and remaining 3½"-wide muslin strips for the background (pieces 2, 3, 5, 6, 8, 9, 11, and 12). These small pieces may become slightly off-grain, but this will not impact the outcome of the quilt. Make 40 paper-pieced trees and separate them into two stacks of 20 each.

3. Sew a 1½" homespun square to one end of each remaining 1½" x 2½" muslin rectangle. Separate the units into two stacks of 40 each. Press the seams toward the muslin for the units in one stack and label this stack A. Press the seams in the opposite direction for the units in the second stack and label this stack B.

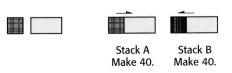

Stack A
Make 40.

Stack B
Make 40.

4. Arrange one 2¼" x 3½" muslin rectangle, one 1½" x 3½" muslin rectangle, a paper-pieced tree from step 2, and one unit each from stack A and stack B as shown. Lay out 20 units with an A segment on the top and a B segment on the bottom, and 20 units with the A and B segments reversed. Sew the muslin rectangles, tree, and A and B units together; press. Make 20 of each unit.

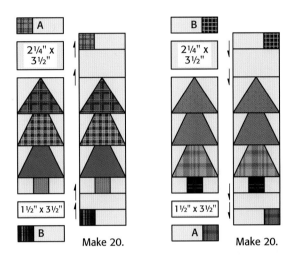

Make 20. Make 20.

ASSEMBLING THE BLOCKS

Sew a tree unit to opposite sides of each cabin/nine-patch unit as shown; press. Make 20 blocks.

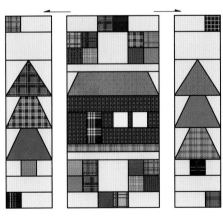

Make 20.

ASSEMBLING THE QUILT

1. Arrange the blocks in five rows of four blocks each, referring to the quilt plan below for guidance.

2. Sew the blocks together into rows. Press the seams in opposite directions from row to row.

3. Sew the rows together; press.

FINISHING THE QUILT

1. Divide the backing fabric crosswise into two equal pieces. Remove the selvage and sew the pieces together to make a single backing piece with one horizontal seam.

2. Layer the quilt top, batting, and backing; baste. (Professional machine quilters prefer to receive the quilt unbasted.)

3. Quilt as desired by hand or machine. I quilted an allover design of waves and swirls on this quilt.

4. Referring to pages 77–78 of "Tips and Techniques," use the 2¼"-wide homespun strips to bind your quilt.

5. Add a hanging sleeve and a label as described on pages 78–79.

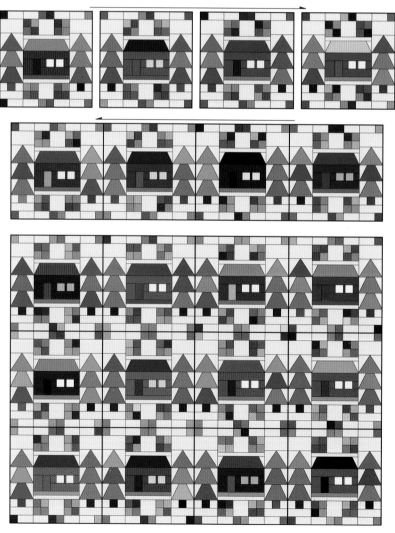

Quilt Plan

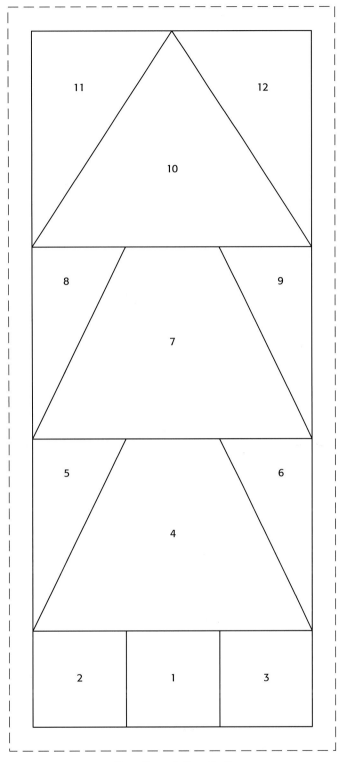

Tree Foundation Unit
Make 40.

THE SATURDAY MARKET

Come Saturdays in Eugene, Oregon, the park streets across from the courthouse are transformed into an open-air market where artisans sell jewelry, clothing, toys, and furniture. Musicians play, and farmers offer up fresh produce, organic meats, seeds, flowers, jams, and jellies. It's a colorful, lively marketplace that includes a quirky water fountain with a metal sculpture of jumping fish. It is common to see many colorful characters in tie-dye who wear business clothes and carry Palm Pilots during the week! "The Saturday Market" has the aura of the marketplace—a lively spirit that makes you smile and a playfulness that is irresistible. To reflect this mood, I used batik fabrics, but theme fabrics—such as holiday or Americana—would be appropriate too. Avoid stripes for the bow-tie portion of the block.

MATERIALS

Yardage amounts are based on 42"-wide fabric.

- 1½ yards of magenta-pink speckled print for blocks and sashing*
- 1 yard of yellow-orange print for blocks
- ⅝ yard of olive green marbled print for blocks
- ⅝ yard of blue medium-scale print for sashing
- ⅝ yard of purple medium-scale print for sashing
- ⅝ yard *total* of assorted green and yellow prints for sashing
- 3 yards of fabric for backing
- ½ yard of magenta print for binding
- 54" x 66" piece of batting

This yardage can be a combination of fat quarters, fat eighths, and/or scraps.

CUTTING

All cutting instructions include ¼"-wide seam allowances.

From the yellow-orange print, cut:

3 strips, 5½" x 42"; crosscut into 16 squares, 5½" x 5½"

4 strips, 3½" x 42"; crosscut into 32 rectangles, 3½" x 4¼"

From the olive green marbled print, cut:

3 strips, 5½" x 42"; crosscut into 16 squares, 5½" x 5½"

From the magenta-pink speckled print, cut:

13 strips, 2⅜" x 42"; crosscut 7 strips into 128 rectangles, 2" x 2⅜". Set the remaining strips aside.

8 strips, 2" x 42"

Finished quilt size: 48" × 60" ■ Finished block size: 12" × 15" (includes sashing)

Pieced and machine quilted by Sheila Sinclair Snyder.

From the blue medium-scale print, cut:
4 strips, 2" x 42"
3 strips, 2⅜" x 42"

From the purple medium-scale print, cut:
4 strips, 2" x 42"
3 strips, 2⅜" x 42"

From the assorted green and yellow prints, cut a *total* of:
128 rectangles, 2" x 2⅜"

From the magenta print, cut:
6 strips, 2¼" x 42"

MAKING THE BLOCKS
You need 16 Bow-Tie blocks to construct this quilt.

1. Draw a diagonal line on the wrong side of each 5½" yellow-orange square. Place a marked square right sides together with each 5½" olive green square. Sew ¼" from each side of the drawn line. Cut on the drawn line; press. Make 32.

Make 32.

2. Mark an 8" (or larger) square ruler with painter's tape. Place the vertical tape line at the 3½" mark, with the tape just outside the line so that you can see the line clearly. Place the horizontal tape line at the 4¼" mark in the same way. Note the ¼" seam-allowance intersections on the top-right and bottom-left corners of the tape-marked rectangle.

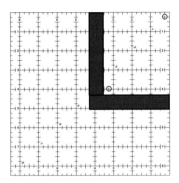

DESIGNER'S TIP
I circle the ¼" seam-allowance marks on my plastic ruler with a white correction pen. This helps me identify the marks quickly and accurately each time. The circles can be easily removed later with a fingernail.

3. Square up each unit from step 1 to 3½" x 4¼" by aligning the diagonal seam of the unit with the ¼" seam-allowance intersections you've identified on the ruler. Note that all edges of the unit fall outside the taped-off area on the ruler. Trim away the right and top edges of the unit. Turn and reposition the ruler, aligning the ¼" seam-allowance intersections with the seam of the unit and aligning the tape with the trimmed edges of the

unit as shown. Trim the remaining sides of the unit. The units will be slightly off-grain, so handle them carefully.

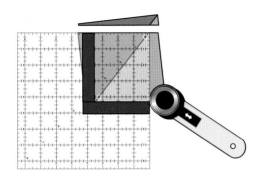

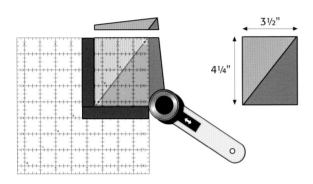

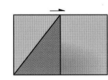

4. Sew a 3½" x 4¼" yellow-orange rectangle to each unit from step 3 as shown; press. Make 32.

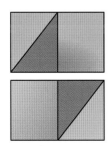 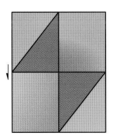

Make 32.

5. Arrange and sew two units from step 4 together as shown; press. Make 16 blocks.

Make 16.

ADDING THE SASHING

1. Sew a 2"-wide magenta speckled strip to a 2"-wide blue strip along one long edge; press. Make four strip sets. Crosscut the strip sets into 16 segments, 8" wide.

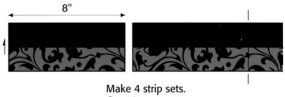

Make 4 strip sets.
Cut 16 segments.

2. Sew a 2"-wide magenta speckled strip to a 2"-wide purple strip along one long edge; press. Make four strip sets. Crosscut the strip sets into 16 segments, 8" wide.

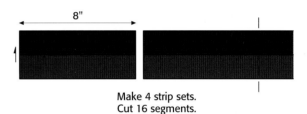

Make 4 strip sets.
Cut 16 segments.

3. Sew a 2⅜"-wide magenta speckled strip to a 2⅜"-wide blue strip along one long edge; press. Make three strip sets. Crosscut the strip sets into 16 segments, 6½" wide.

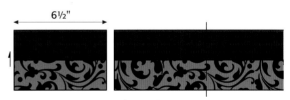

Make 3 strip sets.
Cut 16 segments.

4. Sew a 2⅜"-wide magenta speckled strip to a 2⅜"-wide purple strip along one long edge; press. Make three strip sets. Crosscut the strip sets into 16 segments, 6½" wide.

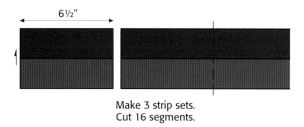

6½"

Make 3 strip sets.
Cut 16 segments.

5. Sew each 2" x 2⅜" green or yellow rectangle to a 2" x 2⅜" magenta speckled rectangle along the longer edge as shown; press. Make 128 pairs. Divide the pairs randomly into two stacks. Make 32 four-patch units from one stack as shown; press. Make 32 four-patch units from the remaining stack, paying careful attention to the placement of the magenta rectangles as shown.

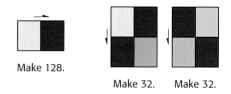

Make 128.

Make 32.   Make 32.

6. Arrange one Bow-Tie block, one segment each from steps 1–4 (with magenta strips facing inward), and two four-patch units from each stack from step 5, deliberately assessing for contrast, harmony, and a good mix of fabric. Lay out 16 blocks.

7. Sew the block, segments, and four-patch units into rows. Press the seams in eight blocks as shown. Press the seams in the remaining eight blocks in the opposite direction.

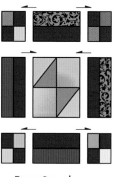

Press 8 as shown.
Press 8 in reverse.

Make 16.
Do not press block.

8. Sew the rows together. Do not press; you will press these seams later.

ASSEMBLING THE QUILT

1. Separate the blocks into two stacks according to how they have been pressed.

2. Drawing alternately from each stack, lay out the blocks in a visually pleasing arrangement of four rows of four blocks each. Refer to the photo on page 67 and the quilt plan on page 71 for guidance.

3. Sew the blocks into rows, pressing the seams of each block as you go. Alternate pressing the seam allowances down for one block and up for the next. When you've finished the rows, press the seams in opposite directions from row to row.

4. Sew the rows together; press.

FINISHING THE QUILT

1. Divide the backing fabric crosswise into two equal pieces. Remove the selvage and sew the pieces together to make a single backing piece with one horizontal seam.

2. Layer the quilt top, batting, and backing; baste. (Professional machine quilters prefer to receive the quilt unbasted.)

3. Quilt as desired by hand or machine. I quilted over the entire surface in fun folk-art designs with a lively variegated thread to match the personality of the quilt.

4. Referring to pages 77–78 of "Tips and Techniques," use the 2¼"-wide magenta print strips to bind your quilt.

5. Add a hanging sleeve and a label as described on pages 78–79.

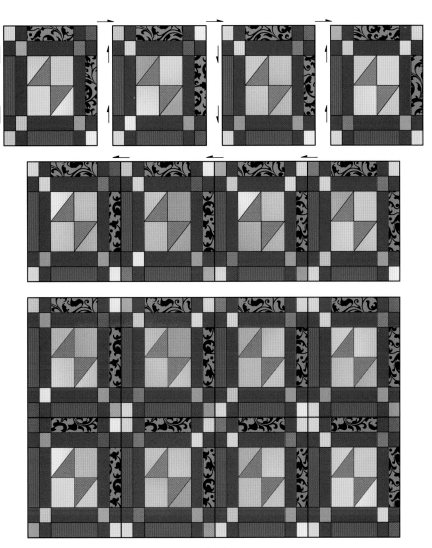

Quilt Plan

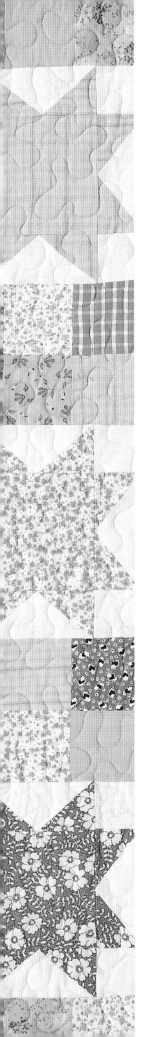

TIPS AND TECHNIQUES

This section gives you some basic tools to complete the various quilts in this book. If you are a beginner, I think you'll find this information especially helpful. If you are a more experienced quiltmaker, you may also want to browse through these pages; I often find that someone else's way of working provides a good new tip or two.

BASIC NEEDLE-TURN APPLIQUÉ

This technique will help you complete the appliqué blocks in "Pathway to Paradise" (page 14).

1. Referring to the project instructions, trace the entire appliqué pattern onto stiff paper. (The dull side of a sheet of freezer paper makes an excellent choice.) Transfer the center horizontal and vertical lines to use as registration marks for placing the appliqué on the background fabric.

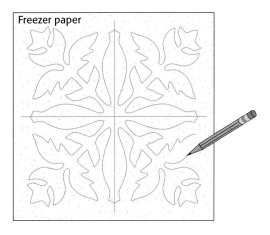

Freezer paper

2. Cut out the paper pattern directly on the traced lines.

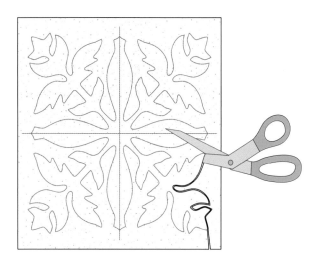

3. Position the pattern on the right side of the desired appliqué fabric. If possible, place the pattern "on point" (on the diagonal) on the fabric. This gives you the greatest amount of bias on the appliqué edge, which will help you needle turn the edges more easily.

4. Trace the pattern onto the right side of the appliqué fabric with a water-soluble marker or mechanical pencil. This line marks the edge you will turn under and stitch. Avoid using a chalk marker for this task, because it will not withstand the repeated handling your piece will receive as you sew.

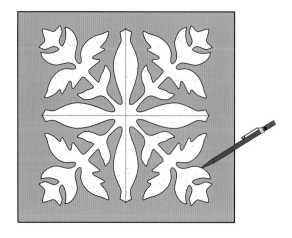

5. Cut out the fabric shape, allowing a generous ¼" seam allowance. You will trim this seam allowance further during the appliqué process.

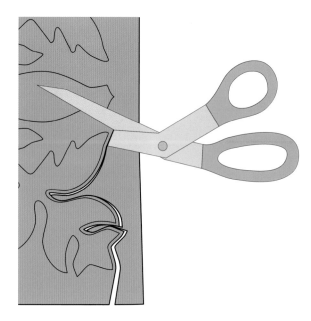

6. Prepare the background fabric by folding it in half both vertically and horizontally, and pressing gently to mark the midpoint. Note that the background piece is cut oversized to compensate for any drawing up that may happen as you stitch.

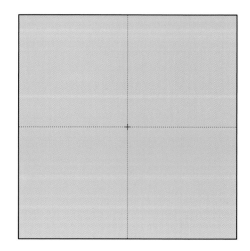

7. Position the appliqué piece on the background fabric, matching the centers and any other registration marks. Roughly baste the appliqué piece in place.

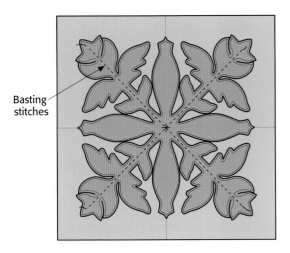

Basting stitches

8. Thread a sharp, fine needle with a single strand of thread that matches the color of the appliqué piece. Knot the thread at one end. Choose a place to begin on the appliqué piece. (A straight edge or gentle curve makes a good place to start.) You'll be working a small section at a time. Roll the edge of the fabric under to the marked stitching line. Finger-press and trim the seam allowance if necessary.

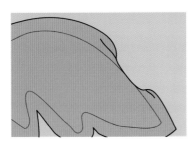

9. Bring your needle from the back of the background fabric to the front, catching just a few threads of the rolled edge of the appliqué. Pull the thread through completely. Reenter the background fabric at the exact point that the needle emerged from the appliqué piece, slightly under the appliqué's rolled edge.

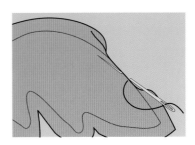

10. Repeat the basic stitch, working your way around the outline of the appliqué shape. The stitches should be approximately ⅛" in length and may be even smaller for intricate shapes. Trim the seam allowance as needed, and turn the edge of the fabric piece under with the needle as you sew. Clip the curves and points as you go.

11. Finish by making two tiny stitches on the back of the block. Take a third stitch and pull the needle through the loop to make a knot. Remove the basting and any remaining visible markings. Follow the project instructions to square up the block to the correct size.

CHAIN PIECING

This efficient technique saves both time and thread when you must sew lots of identical seams and pieces. I recommend it for piecing the stars in "Highly Huggable" (page 47), but you can use it whenever you must sew many identical pieces, units, or blocks.

1. Place the two pieces that you wish to sew right sides together and pin if desired. Prepare all like units at the same time.

2. Stack the prepared units with the same piece on top. Place the stack at your sewing machine, with the edge that you wish to sew turned to face the needle.

3. Fold a small scrap of fabric—often called a thread saver—and sew it from raw edge to raw edge. (This helps keep the machine from "eating" the edges of the first pieces sewn.) Without lifting the presser foot, feed the first unit under the foot. Sew from raw edge to raw edge. Stop sewing, but don't clip the thread.

4. Work your way through the stack, feeding units through the machine. When you have stitched the last seam, remove the "chain" from the machine and clip the threads between the sewn units.

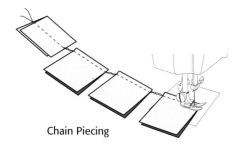

Chain Piecing

BASIC PAPER PIECING

You'll love this method—also called foundation piecing—for assembling the tree units in "Ponderosa Retreat" (page 59).

1. Copy or trace the paper-piecing pattern as directed in the project instructions. Trim away the excess paper on the dashed line, leaving the outer ¼" seam allowance intact.

2. Equip your sewing machine with a fresh new needle and set the stitch length so it is slightly smaller than you normally use for piecing. The smaller stitch will perforate the paper nicely to allow for easy removal later.

3. Turn the pattern over so the printed side is face down. Holding the pattern up to a light source, position the fabric for piece 1 right side up over area 1 on the pattern. Make sure the fabric is large enough to cover the area completely, including a ¼" seam allowance.

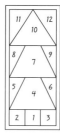

4. Place fabric piece 2 on piece 1, right sides together. (Check to be sure that fabric 2 will cover area 2 when it is stitched and pressed.) Pin if necessary and flip the pattern over so that the printed side is visible and the fabric pieces are on the underside.

5. Stitch on the line between areas 1 and 2. Turn the pattern over and trim away the excess fabric to leave an approximate ¼" seam allowance. Flip piece 2 into position and finger-press (or iron) it onto the paper foundation.

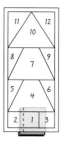

6. Continue adding pieces in numerical order until the paper pattern is covered and the unit is completed; press.

7. Trim the edges of the unit even with the edge of the paper pattern, leaving the outer seam allowances intact. Some quilters prefer to remove paper foundations only after the units have been joined, but for "Ponderosa Retreat" I removed the paper before sewing the paper-pieced units into the blocks. Tweezers work well for carefully removing stubborn pieces.

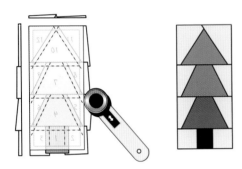

BINDING YOUR QUILT

A well-chosen and well-applied binding gives your quilt a nicely finished edge. I typically use a binding made from 2¼"-wide strips. I choose this size because I like the look of the finished binding, and because the size feels right in my hands as I am working.

1. Cut the number of binding strips as described in the project instructions. (The required number of strips can be determined by totaling the four sides—the perimeter—of the quilt, adding approximately 10" for turning corners and seams, and dividing the total by 42", which is the approximate width of the fabric.)

2. Piece the binding strips together with angled seams. Press the seam allowances open.

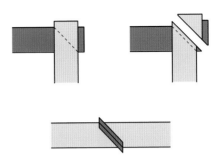

3. Press the binding in half lengthwise, wrong sides together. Cut one end of the binding at a 45° angle, fold under ¼", and press firmly to crease.

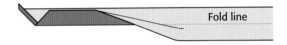

Fold line

4. Trim the excess batting and backing even with the edge of the quilt top.

5. Align the raw edges of the folded binding with the raw edge of the quilt top. Beginning several inches from a corner and approximately 5" or more from the angled end of the binding, sew the binding to the quilt using a scant ⅜" seam allowance. If your binding strips are wider or narrower than 2¼", you may need to adjust the seam allowance slightly. Also be aware that high-loft battings fill the binding more and require smaller seam allowances.

6. Stop stitching ¼" from the first corner of the quilt and backstitch. Remove the quilt from the machine.

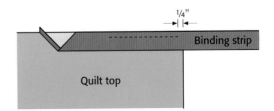

¼"

Binding strip

Quilt top

7. Fold the binding straight up as shown, parallel with the adjacent unfinished edge of the quilt. Fold the binding down along this edge to form a pleat, aligning the folded edge of the binding even with the raw edge of the quilt.

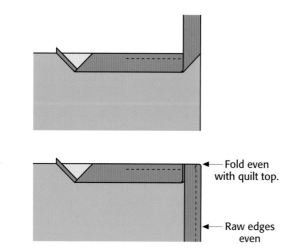

← Fold even with quilt top.

← Raw edges even

8. Continue stitching the binding, turning corners as described. Stop stitching approximately 12" from the starting point of the binding and backstitch. Remove the quilt from the machine.

9. Lay the remaining unbound edge of the quilt on a flat surface. Unfold both ends of the binding strip. Fold the end of the strip and butt it against the starting end of the strip as shown. Press the crease.

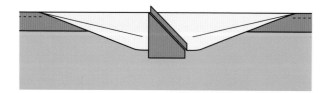

10. Pull the binding away from the quilt and join the strips with machine or hand stitching; use the pressed creases as the stitching line.

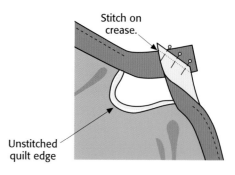

Stitch on crease.

Unstitched quilt edge

11. Check that the binding length is correct, trim the seam allowance to ¼", and press the seam open.

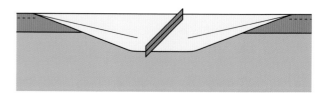

12. Complete the seam to attach the remaining binding to the quilt.

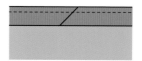

13. Fold the binding to the back of the quilt. A miter will form at each corner. Secure the binding with a blind or hem stitch so that its folded edge covers the machine stitching line. Take a stitch or two in each corner to secure the mitered folds on both the front and back of the quilt.

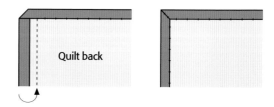

Quilt back

MAKING A REMOVABLE HANGING SLEEVE

You never know when you'll want to display your quilt on a wall or at a show. Be ready with this quilt-friendly method for hanging your work. Unlike some other methods, this one allows you to remove the sleeve at any time, since it is not sewn into the binding.

1. Cut a strip of fabric 8" and the width of your quilt. You may need to sew strips together to get a strip of the correct length.

2. Turn and press under a ½" hem on each end of the strip. Repeat, and then stitch the hem.

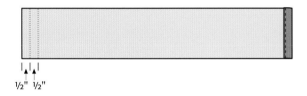

½" ½"

3. Fold the strip lengthwise, right sides together, and sew the strip into a long tube with a ¼" seam. Turn the tube right side out and press flat.

4. Slip-stitch the top edge of the sleeve to the quilt backing just below the bound edge. Slip-stitch the bottom edge of the hanging sleeve to the quilt backing. You can remove the sleeve if necessary since it is not sewn into the binding.

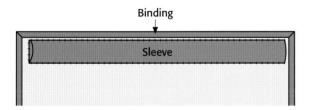

Binding

Sleeve

ADDING A QUILT LABEL

It is very important to label each quilt. A label gives you an opportunity to document the quilt for the future and to include a sentimental message if you choose. I often piece my label into the backing of the quilt; the quilting ensures that the label can't become unattached. At other times I appliqué the label to the backing after the quilt is finished.

Be sure your label includes the name of the quilt; the name of the maker; the city, state, and date; and—if applicable—the name of the quilter and the quilt's recipient. Include any other interesting information to help document the quilt.

Labels can be embroidered, cross-stitched, printed on the computer, written with permanent fabric markers, or any combination of the above. Be creative in adding this finishing touch to your quilt!

ABOUT THE AUTHOR

When the repairman tells her to start looking for another sewing machine, Sheila Sinclair Snyder has learned to listen up; she has already worn out two sewing machines! Sewing and quilting are not just hobbies for Sheila, but a lifestyle. The quilts keep multiplying and the stash keeps growing . . . along with the books, magazines, and patterns. She believes there is always another idea developing, a new technique to try, a class to take, a retreat to investigate, or a Web site to check!

Well-known for her fine quality long-arm machine quilting, Sheila also teaches classes in machine quilting and quilt construction. Integrating her first career as an occupational therapist, Sheila incorporates ergonomics for quilters into her classes, combining these two interests. She has two grown children, Matthew and Julia, and lives with her husband, Elvin, in Eugene, Oregon.